ECOLOGY AND HUMAN WELL-BEING
Nature and Society in Himachal Pradesh

Ecology and Human Well-being

Nature and Society in Himachal Pradesh

Raghubir Singh Pirta

Published for Institute of Integrated Himalayan Studies,
(UGC Centre of Excellence), H.P. University, Shimla

SHIPRA

ISBN: 81-7541-354-9

First Published in India in 2007

Ecology and Human Well-being:
Nature and Society in Himachal Pradesh

Published by:
SHIPRA PUBLICATIONS
115-A, Vikas Marg, Shakarpur
Delhi-110092, INDIA
Phone: 91-11-65277210, 91-11-22500954
Fax: 91-11-22458662
E-mail: info@shiprapublications.com
www.shiprapublications.com

To
my
affectionate mother
and
caring father

Foreword

Dr. R.S. Pirta's book "*Ecology and Human Well-being: Nature and Society in Himachal Pradesh*", though deals with the Ecology and society of Himachal Pradesh, yet it is of national and global importance. The mountains in India and all over the world have been the victims of materialistic civilization, which aims at converting Nature to cash. The land use of the hills have been for earning revenue by the respective governments by eliminating the natural vegetation and raising commercial forests—the timber mines. The timber species—the conifers deplete soil and suck water. This led to impoverishment of soil and the local population. The government's vision was to popularize luxury tourism, which would bring money. But the basic principle of tourism, maintenance of scenic beauty was ignored, by constructing roads, which created scars on the hill-slopes.

Dr. Pirta—a son of Himalaya has combined his experiences with field studies, which he carried on while walking in the villages. Market economy, which is based upon the exploitation of nature and the labour of toiling masses, has made the magnificent Himalaya, a cursed land. Our ancestors had worshipped Himalaya and established the shrines on the tops of hills from where the rivers originated. They valued the hills for water. Felling of trees and construction of roads has created the scarcity of water in the hills itself.

Fortunately the common masses in the hills raised voice against felling of the trees and as a result of their constant struggle against tree felling through Chipko movement, the government of India put a ban on felling of green trees above 1000 meters altitude.

Twenty first century has come with the message of water-crisis, which has been accelerated with the rise in temperature. There is an urgent need to cover the Himalayan slopes with trees giving food (nuts, edible seeds, oil seeds, flowering trees for honey and seasonal fruits), fodder, fibre, fertilizer (leaf fertilizer) trees and a few trees for timber and fuel. The entire population of Himalaya should be given employment in planting and protecting of trees. This is the great task of defence of the country against hunger, thirst and disease. I am sure that those, who care for the welfare of society shall seriously go through Dr. Pirta's book and dedicate themselves in making India—a country of *vandemataram* singer's dream—*sujalam, sufalam, shasya shyamalam*, good water, good fruits and ever green.

12.9.2006 **Sunderlal Bahuguna**

Prologue

Dr. R.S. Pirta has explored the complex man-nature relationships essential for the survival of all living beings. Though the study is an attempt to resolve environmental issues that pertains to Himachal Pradesh, the explanations reflect a deeper global understanding of the author.

The primary objective of this study was to raise issues that are significant in taking policy decisions at various levels, a dialogue in which IIHS have the main stake in the Western Himalayan region. *Ecology and Human Well-being* concentrates on issues of environment endured by various sections of society in Himachal Pradesh. Furthermore, the wide experience of the author with eminent environmentalists in India and participation in ecological projects has helped Dr. Pirta to comprehend the relevance of the local issues in broader context, which is the significant aspect of this volume.

In brief, the first half of the report explains the major issues and problems in the three chapters: life and its support system, ecology and sustainability, and social aspects of water, forest and land. The second half of the study introduces some approaches and solutions related to sustainable development. Beginning with the diversity of views it is followed by evidence on cooperative relationships in three scenarios—the primate societies, the natives of Himalayas and the institution of deity.

In the holistic approach, socio-cognitive factors are very important and require a fine balance of myth and reality. This is particularly true for Himachal Pradesh where myth and reality live in the institutions of the deity. These institutions integrate physical, social and mental aspects of the nature and society in human psyche where sustainable way of life flourishes.

December 16, 2006
Shimla

Prof. Yoginder Verma
Director
Institute of Integrated Himalayan Studies
H.P. University, Shimla

Preface

The realization in the Millennium Ecosystem Assessment (MA 2005) that the well-being of all people is important and is linked with the health of the eco-system is a phenomenal change. Since it has been expressed at the global level through an endeavour of science, this is a unique event. Furthermore, the emphasis is to link the ecosystem services with quality of social institutions as well as quality of interventions taking place within them.

The aim of this report is to present the existing state of the selective social and environmental issues in the northwest Himalaya as perceived by the people including scientists, politicians, planners and other intelligentsia. Although the emphasis is to develop a holistic view of nature and society, the other two interactions—the human dominance over its environment and the natural constraints on the social system—cannot be undermined.

Since the understanding of the surrounding physical and social systems is dependent upon the cognitive and mental factors, an attribute of human species, there are chances of subjectivity or bias. The criterion to rectify this bias has to be worked out by human beings themselves. This is the biggest dilemma when we talk about ecology and sustainability. Ecology refers to the relationship among the elements (natural and manmade) of the ecosystem whereas sustainability is the human constraint to maintain these relationships for our own as well as the survival of future generations. This human constraint is almost entirely defined by human beings themselves as far as the most dominant views of environment are concerned.

A controversial problem that often figures in environmental debates is the limited land area and the growth of the human population. It is in this area particularly that even the most venerable minds have fallen to Malthusian fallacy. They grossly undermine the human cognitive competence to solve problems. All limits of decency are crossed to reduce the Darwinian fitness, but at the same time a large industry thrives by increasing the libidinal impulses of people. In such a scenario, the demographic profile of Himachal Pradesh makes academicians complement its peasantry.

Although the limitless demands of humans may be an important factor contributing to large number of environmental problems, the most learned section of society grossly undermines it. Even writers from developing societies are entrapped by materialistic fallacy—the happiness lies in the acquisition of more and more material goods—undermining the role of mental states in it. Moreover, they engage in vociferous campaign to denigrate own culture and society, little realizing that the silent folks in hilly terrain of Himachal Pradesh are socially the most progressive in India.

This brings us to the issue of poverty and its presumed negative relationship with environment. It is rare to find writers who have negated this relationship, but it is difficult to ascertain the nature of its role in lowering the pace of development. It is uniquely in this case that the planners, politicians and the enforcing agencies, by neglecting the role of psychological and social factors, have severe drawback. Rather they seem to propagate the colonization of mind of local people by the materialistic policies of developed world.

There appears to be lack of sensitivity in our policies regarding scientific findings on one hand and the needs of the people on the other hand. An example of this split is construction of the large dams. The policy makers in this case have overlooked the science of ecology as well as the miseries of the displaced people. At the same time, emphasis has been to compel Himachal Pradesh to earn more money by exploiting its forest resources. A major challenge is to understand the dynamic relationship between forest, water and land, especially in the context of watershed development programmes. It is here that the natives of Himalayas were able to persuade the most reluctant politicians for the sustainable use of forests through the Chipko or hug-the-tree movement.

In order to understand the relationship between society and nature in Himachal Pradesh several contemporary theoretical viewpoints are also introduced to grasp the complexity of the social-system and eco-system. Still more important is the role of human cognitive and mental factors in mediating the complexity of these two systems. Many now consider the cooperative nature of society as an important factor in sustainable development. In this context it is important to explore the biological origin of cooperation so that there is a sound theoretical basis for an affectionate human group.

Acknowledgements

This was a rewarding reminiscence of my walks in the lovely terrain of Himachal. Several colleagues in the H.P. University were companions for short or long time. My experiences enriched with their insights. Professor L.R. Verma, the Honourable Vice-Chancellor of the University and the Professor Yoginder Verma, the Director of the IIHS were among those with whom I had long conversations at the entrance to this institution. It is on their insistence that the volume has come out.

Those colleagues from whom I have learned a lot include Chetan Singh, Laxman Singh Thakur and Vidya Sagar Negi. There are others whose ideas I have incorporated directly in the text do not need mention here. Some of these social activists are continuing the arduous task. A few had silently passed away.

Above all, the influence of Shri Sunderlal Bahuguna and Shrimati Vimla Bahuguna may find reflection on these pages, if not, perhaps due to my misperception. The same may be true for Professor Madhav Gadgil, a well-known ecologist of India who in his own way asked me to stand up. Gandhian social workers and Chipko friends has always inspired me. All this needed high self-esteem that my family and friends built in me for a better cause. What I have learned from them is the core of this report since I know very well that this is what they expect from the coming generation.

I express my sincere thanks to Shri D. Kumar, Shipra Publications and Shri Prem Verma, IIHS for their help in bringing out this volume.

R.S. Pirta

Contents

List of Boxes

Lists of Figures

Lists of Tables

1

Life and its Support System

The moment life emerges from its constituent matter, it assumes the role of an entity interacting with the surrounding milieu in diverse ways. This entity is termed as an organism, a living thing. Its constituent elements, from which the organism emerges, form the environment or the life support system. This life support system not only comprises of essential living and non-living elements of the constituent matter, but it also includes spatially distributed invisible molecules. These molecules are densely packed as the earth, loosely connected together as the sea or water and in the form of rare medium, they constitute the earth's atmosphere. There are several other bodies in the space at variable distances that visibly or invisibly affect the process of life on earth.

Nature's Driving Forces

Essentially, an organism is self-changing. It is also capable of modifying the environment. In return, the environment also affects the organism. These interactions revolve around two kinds of activities. The first is to survive over a period, the life span of the organism, and secondly to replicate itself, the driving force of the organic or biological evolution.

In carrying out these two important functions, namely survival and reproduction, an organism engages in various kinds of interactions with the constituents of the environment. The interactions taking place in time and space having certain predictable patterns develop into relationships. These relationships involve the individuals of its own kind, the members of other species, and the non-living milieu constituting objects and inorganic molecules distributed in the space. The science of ecology explores these relationships supporting the web of life which forms the ecosystem. In fact, the ecosystem provides essential services for human well-being (Box 1.1).

In a specific environment, only particular kind of interactions occur. The organisms distribute themselves spatially according to their specific nature and the features of the surrounding environment. The organism can thus perform only certain interactions with the surrounding milieu or terrain. These specific transactions of the organism are the niche whereas the terrain forms its habitat. Largely these transactions are innate. Though, these adaptations have taken millions of years but there is scope for adaptive modifications through experience or learning during the lifetime of the organism.

Evolving Consciousness

The organism's relationships with the environment assume purposive nature, to the extent that they optimize the survival of the organism. This may be extended to groups of similar organisms, to the members of same species but forming different group, and the whole life support system. In evolutionary terms, these relationships are known as group survival, survival of the species and the Gaia, respectively. They form some of the most challenging and controversial problems in the biological evolution of social behaviour.

Box 1.1: Ecosystem and society

"The Millennium Ecosystem Assessment is an outstanding example of the sort of international scientific and political cooperation that is needed to further the cause of sustainable development. ...I call on Member States to help provide the necessary financial support for the Millennium Ecosystem Assessment and to become actively engaged in it."

Kofi A. Annan, *We the Peoples: The Role of the United Nations in the 21st Century. April 2000*

The human beings are organized in a heterogeneous group spread all over the Earth's surface. Efforts for homogenization in past were mainly due to knowledge seeking journeys of explorers and secondly by the conquests of the rulers to acquire greener pastures. These scenarios when portrayed by the historians generate representations

(*Contd.*)

(*Contd.*)

in the minds that people can comprehend. The present processes of homogenization are mammoth. They are invisible, fearsome and apparently unpredictable. The familiar term globalisation best describes these processes and they are mainly identified with the economic activities of the large organizations.

But this is not the entire story. There are efforts to make the planet Earth a living entity where all human beings cooperate with each other. The Millennium Ecosystem Assessment (MA) completed in less than four years in March 2005 is viewed as the living example of such a cooperative enterprise. The scientists from all over the world united to highlight the state of various kinds of ecosystem services in the context of human well-being. These scientists isolated the direct and indirect drivers responsible for changes in the ecosystem. The factors such as habitat loss, climate change, invasions by species, overexploitation of resources and pollution of air, water and land are the direct drivers of ecosystem. There are however various social factors, the changes in population, economic enterprises, socio-political activities, religious and cultural aspects and the innovations of science and technology, which indirectly change the ecosystem.

It is also important to note that the human well-being is dependent on material welfare, health, good social relations, security, and freedom. Perhaps material scientists largely considered these qualities important only for their interests (e.g., freedom in pursuing their research interests) though there may be a few radicals. Whereas social relationships needed for security and freedom in various spheres of life are considered by these scientists as less significant activities confined to arm-chair thinkers and those engaged in the non-scientific pursuits.

In all probability, the evolution of consciousness changed the whole scenario of the organic evolution. Particularly the assumed purposive nature of an organism's relationships with the environment took a new turn. In other words, after the evolution of consciousness, the elusiveness of the purpose hidden in these relationships has become an extremely important voluntary enterprise for the individual as well as for the group. The main thrust of this purposive enterprise is in the development and manipulation of selfish interests of individuals and its kin. But the cooperative enterprise seems to be a more fundamental principle in the evolution of the life support system.

Therefore, the important problem is to enhance those relationships in a society which are essential for survival of the life support system. The society is a mediator between the organism and the environment. It seems that the cooperative relationships maintain or increase the resiliency of these systems, whereas selfishness makes them vulnerable. This is fundamental to any kind of human developmental effort as it involves social institutions. Particularly, it is related more with the social relationships occurring within the society than with the relationships of the organism with material environment.

Today scientists have a deeper knowledge about the molecules of material. However, our understanding of the basic structure of the human society and the constituent groups is very shallow. The latter kinds of interactions were a predominant focus of enquiry with the advent of materialism. There is however a far greater need to understand the social and cognitive nature of human evolution and to discern the ways in which it affects interactions and relationships within a society.

Socio-cognitive Revolution

Human beings have broken the evolutionary constraints through their cognitive revolution. For example, the membership of modern human groups now seldom needs the physical presence of the individual, a prerequisite in the natural groups of all the animal species, including primitive human groups. Secondly, the interactions within the group take place in highly symbolic terms in the minds of its members and it is stored in the episodic memory. And the third important change is that the group is not restricted by time and space limits. Lastly, the biological evolution is coming more and more under the control of cultural evolution, an artifact of the socio-cognitive processes. It is through the cultural evolution that the biological evolution finds its expression (Box 1.2).

This has both positive and negative consequences in the context of sustainability, as we will try to understand in a 'remote' Himalayan region like Himachal Pradesh. For example, consider the terms remoteness, alienation and marginalisation. With the advancement of technology, the product of socio-cognitive revolution, the physical component of these terms has hardly any meaning. These terms are however more meaningful from social and cognitive side. For example, the societies of these regions may continue to live in remoteness, isolation and face marginalisation, but they have become easily approachable and are amenable to manipulation by the developed world, through various dimensions of power. Unless affected groups realize the importance of socio-cognitive revolution, these societies would continue to take refuge in the artifacts of the advanced groups. The changes in these groups would be perceived as symptoms of deterioration of cognition.

Box 1.2: Myth and reality

Penelope Chetwode in *Kulu: The End of the Habitable World* (1972) describes the myth and reality of Himachal Pradesh. She began, "*It is the fashion today, especially among the young, to denigrate the British Raj. Imperialism was a phase in the history of mankind which is now nearly over and personally I think that in the assessment of future historians the Roman, Gupta, and the British Empires will rank high.*"

On the greatness of the British officers who ruled India, the point where I agree with Penelope Chetwode, is that many of them collected the "stores of knowledge" for the humanity. This is the most important point that I would like to stress on in the present essay. Since a new form of imperialism accompanies globalization, which is neither physical nor social, but mental. The above lines of Chetwode contain the hidden message to face it. Although the political leaders of Himachal Pradesh have laid the foundation of basic education in the State, it is imperative that the people of Himachal Pradesh get ready for the great cognitive leap.

While making this leap it is necessary to keep the base intact and build the future with the help of this unique treasure, although it may be full of myths. Creative persons take the help of a myth until they come to know the reality; the myth is rejected when one stumbles upon the reality. These people often come across these transitions between myth and reality. In the wake of such moment Chetwode wrote:

"I leapt from my mule and rushed up the khud just in time to see the first men appear over the brow of a bare brown hill, carrying an enormous red and white standard. Next came the musicians: a few flautists, a few drummers, two men blowing curved 'serpents'—resembling those used in English churches in the eighteenth century—and another two carrying six-foot silver trumpets over their shoulders.

(*Contd.*)

(*Contd.*)

These are so heavy that the musicians have to stand still to blow them and can only do so for about thirty seconds at a time. The flutes play runny tunes, the serpents arpeggios, the drums thrilling rhythms and the great trumpets blare out octaves with such compelling force that I am tempted to apostatise on the spot and throw myself down before the devata: it is real primeval Sare du Printemps stuff which would surely have intoxicated Stravinsky."

Penelope Chetwode traveled the land of Himachal Pradesh on mule back to discover the treasure in the fossilized temples, among the moving gods, and in the recesses of the mind.

This happened in the nineteen sixties. While retracing her own steps in the year 1986, according to the villagers of Deem, on way to the Jalori Pass, "*Penelope Chetwode had invoked the blessings of the local deity with a desire to die in the Himalayas.*" (Shawab, 1996) Her wish was fulfilled. She died at some distance from the village and was cremated there.

Almost a week before her death, I had a chance to have the first and the last interaction with Penelope Chetwode at the Ridge in Shimla. She emphasized on the role of Indian culture and tradition on which there was enormous material that needed a careful interpretation. The predominant contemporary view that had influenced her environmental thinking was the work of Teilhard de Chardin.

Some years ago, the regional director of Unesco in India, Kingston (1998) wondered "*Why, in India we had, from very early times, cave paintings that showed the harmonious coexistence of the human and the natural world. Groves would be set aside for the worship of gods and goddesses, certain plants and animals would be considered sacred and would be protected. Probably it indicated harmony of people with nature.*"

The important point is to increase the storehouse of knowledge. This is the ultimate goal of humanity. There are however proximate needs that necessitate cognitive contribution. I feel this urgency more from the latter standpoint. Our state gazetteers indicate a downward trend. The scenario of research is gloomy. For example the *State of Environment Report—Himachal Pradesh* 2001 could have been a good model for the new generation (Chapter 2; p. 31).

It is clear that the evolution of human species on the planet unleashed a new and rapid process of evolution. Its members first made cognitive representations of the cosmos and now they are ready to colonise some of its other planets. It would be a great mistake to undermine the immense potential of the human cultural evolution where the individuals and the groups are important players. The social power of human groups and creativity of individuals are now pulling the reins of the organic evolution. There is enormous evidence to support that in the past few thousand years the human cultural evolution has left behind the biological evolution that had taken place over millions of years.

Human species, through this new evolution, mainly driven by social and cognitive forces, has assumed the role of the creator, protector and destroyer. It is important to understand how human species assumed these three roles. Perhaps this socio-cognitive revolution has material and non-material basis in the enormous cortical neurons and their infinite emergent mental properties. Sometimes human cognition understands it a single universal consciousness but at other times it takes the dualistic form, the material and the non-material. But these are not old problems of different schools of thought. These issues assume greater significance in the context of a post-modern society which is looking for some new ethics of behaviour with nature (Box 1.3).

Human Responsibility

In this new conceptualization, the interactions taking place between nature and society in any part of the world are being understood in terms of the interactions taking place between the biological and the cultural evolution. But the significant point is that although there are some universal principles, the interactions are constrained by the specificity of the natural habitat and the uniqueness a mental process assumes in that situation. However, the social institutions mediate between the niche (specific physical/mental interactions possible in a habitat) and the unique cognitive solutions. These social institutions are also constrained by organic as well as cultural factors in a specific location.

Box 1.3: Nature of change

One would find it in the poems of Octavio Paz, the Nobel Laureate in literature. In his three poems "Himachal Pradesh" (I – III) Paz makes a metaphoric travel through this Himalayan region. He depicts the gradual loss of human spirituality in favour of a physical existence (Carpenter, 1999). There is a transition from cognition to non-cognition. The grandeur of the landscape of Himachal, as a spiritual paradise, is giving way to materialism. He sees the regression of human cognition to primal state (fulfillment of bodily needs). In such patterns of behaviour the society alienates the self.

The late Prime Minister Indira Gandhi, who was crucial in the formation of Himachal Pradesh as a larger State (the *Vishal Himachal*) would have definitely been dismayed by such a change among the people of the State. Probably this is not the direction that she envisioned. For her, the higher standard of living must be achieved without alienating our people from their heritage and without disposing nature of its beauty, freshness, and purity, essential to our lives. These feelings also find expression in her action towards saving the forests of the Himalayas where she supported the cause of the Chipko Movement (see Appendices 1 & 2).

A person, who is largely unknown, has been perseveringly engaged in his efforts to save the environment and culture in the Himalayas. N. D. Jayal has a vast experience of administration and environment in the Himalayan terrain. Starting his carrier from the remote Kinnaur in Himachal Pradesh he was selected by the then Prime Minister of India, Mrs. Indira Gandhi to head the Forestry and Wildlife Ministry Wing as the Joint Secretary in the Ministry of Agriculture.

In the following years he took up the task of establishing the Department of Environment. He was crucial in developing evaluation methodologies of major projects like the Tehri Dam. After his retirement, as the Director of Natural Heritage Wing of INTACH, N.D. Jayal has continued his efforts to save the Himalaya from the large scale interventions such as 260.5 m high Tehri Dam on the river Bhagirathi.

For example, Himachal Pradesh, due to its location in the western Himalayas has some unique physical aspects (geological, geographical, climatic, biological), moreover, it also has a unique individual and collective component of human cognition. The latter includes the thoughts, beliefs, attitudes and aspirations of the people living in this State. Thus the society in this Himalayan region would have its unique ways of mediating between the relationships of the individual and its surrounding milieu. The cognitive revolution, however, made it possible for experts to intervene directly or indirectly and affect the local decision making process. This is largely the case in the area of agricultural sciences which affect the livelihood of about 92 per cent population in Himachal Pradesh (Box 1.4).

For a study in sustainability, it is therefore important to understand the nature of these relationships toward the life support systems, since our survival, biological and cultural, is dependent upon the survival of the life support system. It is also a mistake to consider that the life support system has only a physical aspect. There are at least three broad dimensions of human survival, namely biological, social and mental. Some may even emphasise a fourth dimension, the spiritual.

The main thrust of the modern developmental process, throughout the world, has been on physical (including biological) aspects by acquiring necessary experience to utilize them for the sake of human species. Other dimensions of life have been overlooked in this process. This is rather a disastrous neglect of the materialists who on one hand use the product of cognitive revolution (science and technology) to appropriate the material resources for human benefit, but on the other hand they seem to deny the special need to understand the holistic purpose of life.

Box 1.4: Agrarian ecosystem

The human societies all over the world have, over the centuries, carved out agrarian ecosystems. They are, however, embedded within the respective larger ecosystems. The human-land relationship within these agro-ecosystems is largely governed by the agricultural sciences. The relationships within these agro-ecosystems need careful consideration, particularly in Himachal Pradesh where agriculture is the main source of livelihood. Often the decision making process overlooks science as well as traditional wisdom, it is the expert power that dominates.

For example, consider the distinction made between the indigenous agro-forestry as a historical system and the propagation of the agro-forestry as a modern strategy of experts developed in the 1980s. In the latter case it is defined as a concept for creating intentional change in the land based production to meet the subsistence needs of farmers

(*Contd.*)

(*Contd.*)

(Denholm & Jodha, 1992). Is the distinction necessary? Quite understandably it is, because only then, one becomes the expert to give his knowledge to farmers. This involves a huge risk at the cost of society and nature.

Consider the use of the concept of 'niche'. Mountains are isolated areas, lack transportation, and vary in climate, geology, flora and fauna. Niche is defined as the 'mountain areas' with greater suitability for specific activities/products as source of 'comparative advantage' (Denholm & Jodha, 1992). The interventions suggested to the farmers are to take benefit of potential for irrigation and hydropower, timber production and horticulture. On this basis it is argued that in Himachal Pradesh 'niche' provides a comparative advantage (Bhatti, Singh, Rathore & Sharma, 1992; Verma & Pratap, 1992).

A more conspicuous example of the expert power of the agricultural scientists is the propagation of potato cultivation in the mountains. The experts consider mountains as special niche for potato cultivation. But the later technological inventions made plains even more appropriate for the potato cultivation. But by the time long stretches of the mountains have been felled, even larger areas had already become barren.

There appears to be a conceptual ambiguity in the use of niche. This should be clear from Odum's (1996) distinction between habitat and niche. Habitat is the address of the organism and niche is what the organism is able to do in that habitat. However, the examples of niche in these studies may not be specific to Himachal, they seems universal to mountain areas. The specificities would include those artifacts over which people of Himachal Pradesh have monopoly due to its habitat features and also due to their cognitive innovations.

Holistic Path

Unless we consciously understand some fundamental questions, which human species is uniquely endowed with, it is not possible to decide where we are heading to; towards life or towards death. Those fundamental questions involve, besides the survival and propagation of the human species and its support system, the decisions related to the quality of our survival and the forethought about the quality of the survival of the coming generations. This is also an extremely selfish human viewpoint.

Since modern human beings have assumed the role of creator, protector and destroyer, they have to realize the significance of this new responsibility. The use of technology has been largely made to exhaust the living and non-living support system of life on this cosmos, but the human responsibility is to use nature's gift of cognition in such a way that our role as creator and protector becomes more conspicuous than as the destroyer. There is a saying in Himachali folklore that the protector is greater than the destroyer.

The holistic science of ecology emphasizes upon those relationships that support life rather than those that are deleterious to life. This is the dimension of sustainability, which is highly purposive in nature and aims at the long-term survival of conscious and unconscious life processes on Mother Earth or Gaia. In order to achieve this, it is imperative to evolve new ethics to direct the relationships in a society for enhancing the life support system. This task at the global level involves the efforts of all the nations to save the Mother Earth or Gaia but it is equally important that the governing policies in small regions like Himachal Pradesh harmonize with this mission (Box 1.5).

Box 1.5: From whole to parts

Human cognitive abilities can immensely enrich the niche by contributing to the repertoire of the habitat specific behaviours. There is however a tendency of dominance or use of power by other group to check it or compete with it. Therefore the "comparative advantage" starts diminishing. To counter the competitive strategies of the other groups there is need for a more superior cognitive innovation, a greater emphasis on more specialization in interactions between the people and their habitat. In other words there is competition between the "specialists" and the more dominant "generalists."

There seems to be a paradox, especially in context of the huge neocortical mass that each individual possesses and its immense potential for cognitive innovations, which is a universal feature. On the other hand, there is a little use of this potential by a majority of population living on the subsistence level. The way to resolve the paradox is perhaps very clear, to make use of this immense potential for "specialization." But to achieve this, the route people choose is from specialists to generalists. Another path is from generalists to specialists.

(Contd.)

(*Contd.*)

This is a path from whole to its parts, which needs experimentation.

An understanding of the global scenario is most important today for people when the cultural evolution has released the human species from its biological constraints. Now the human habitat is not narrow, as it was for the primitive human groups, its extent is the whole earth. If the people of Himachal Pradesh do not want to enlarge their habitat, they may do it at a great risk. Perhaps they do not have enough power to stop the others to graze their habitat. In this sense niche for modern human beings is only beneficial if they take benefit of the cognitive evolution and take a route from generalists to specialists.

People of Himachal Pradesh may choose to remain specialists but they will have to import experts, as is the present scenario. The cost is very heavy. Socially, the people are classified as poor, less developed and some times a burden to the more developed. Take for example watershed management and social forestry schemes. The State is borrowing huge amount of money and expert power even for these comparatively less complex cognitive activities.

Society in Himachal Pradesh

Most of the studies on society and culture in Himachal Pradesh are descriptive and imaginary. However, the data collected in People of India (POI) project provide discrete information on various aspects of the society in Himachal Pradesh. The POI project of the Anthropological Survey of India (1985 to 1992) provides wealth of data on 2,753 communities of India (Singh, 2002). The community means '*samudaya*', it is largely used to signify endogamous caste groups but it also includes caste like structures that do not follow caste norms. Although our mental representations of caste and the behavioural relationships among these community groups have been changing, it still provides significant way of visualizing the cultural diversity in India. According to Singh (2002), the leader of the POI project, "*A community, like an individual, sees its identity at multiple levels in time and space*."

Community was a unit of study in POI project that explored the cultural diversity of the people of India. The original analysis of data on 4,635 communities (in fact there were 2,753 communities but some communities were found in more than one State/Union Territory), 58 communities were added after 1992 so the figure now is 4,693 communities. These data are related to 776 individual items (traits) grouped under 15 broad categories: (1) nomenclature, identity, history, migration, distribution, natural environment, etc., (2) bio-anthropological material, (3) food and food habits, (4) social divisions, hierarchy, and stratification, (5) institution of marriage, (6) family, (7) status of women, (8) life-cycle rituals, (9) occupation and economic activities, (10) mechanism of social controls, (11) religious attributes, (12) art and culture, (13) inter-community linkages, (14) attitude towards development process and its impact, and (15) any other observation of importance concerning life and culture of the community (Box 1.6).

Box 1.6: Himachal Pradesh

Himachal Pradesh is a state of the Indian Union located in the mountains of the western Himalaya. It covers an area of approximately 55,673 square kilometers divided into twelve administrative districts. According to the census of 1991, the total population of the State was a little over 5 million, and in 2001 it crossed 6 million. Men outnumber women by a little margin.

Political organization indicates the influence of geography. Principalities and even smaller administrative entities in pre-British times had, over the centuries, evolved a balance between their resource requirements and the ecosystem from which these resources were obtained. The role of 'village community' has in this context, been considerably important; especially village commons, forests, grazing land and water resources (for an authoritative exposition see Singh, 1998).

Equally important, though less studied, has been the manner in which individual peasant families managed their isolated lives in the tiny and scattered hamlets of the Himalayas where the 'community' was, at times, more a notion than a concrete reality. It was here that the religion, social norms and nature converged to enable the Himalayan peasant to assemble his daily life.

Summarized here is some information that is relevant to Himachal Pradesh. The POI project provides important links between environment, resource endowments and communities and between ecology and community. The information according to regions and eco-cultural zones and distribution of communities and traits characteristic of these communities may be useful to develop hypotheses for future studies at the local level. This is because the investigators are very clear that the regional identity is grounded in objective realities such as ecology, language, culture, ethnicity, and in subjective perception.

The population in a state has no correlation with the number of communities. They are spread in all climatic zones of India (Figure 1.1). The largest concentration of the communities is in the plains (2485), followed by the hilly terrain (1147), plateaux (804), coasts (686), valleys (236), semiarid regions (240), high altitudes (102), deserts (69), and islands (29). The rural setting comprised of most of the communities (60%) whereas the urban areas had only few (8.5%). There were some percentage (28.8%) of communities that lived in urban and rural settings (Box 1.7).

Fig. 1.1: Distribution of communities according to climatic zones

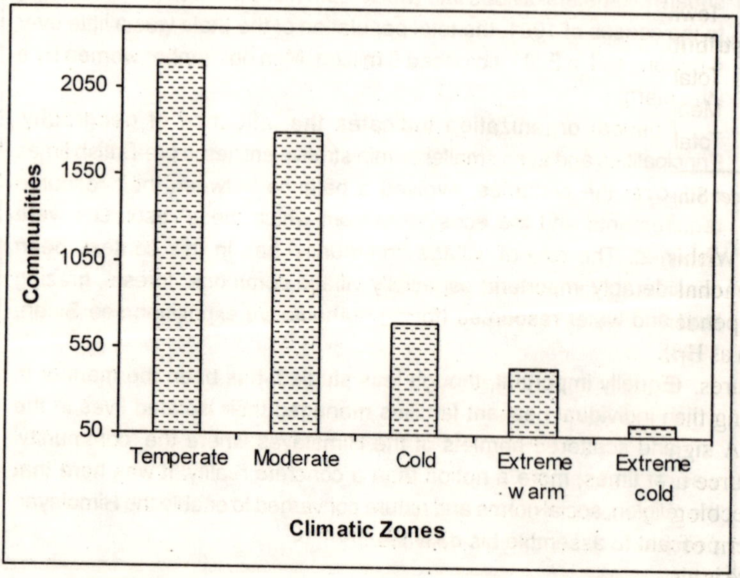

Source: Singh, 2002.

The biological variation among the communities suggests that geographical variable plays a vital role in the gene flow than in the social order. It was found that the people of Himachal Pradesh are similar with the people of Jammu & Kashmir and Uttaranchal. However, the possibility of gene flow cannot be entirely ruled out. Furthermore, the average morphometric features of the people of Himachal Pradesh are somewhat in the middle of the range between those found in Jammu & Kashmir on one side and Punjab and Haryana on the other.

Box 1.7: People of India (POI) Project

Anthropological Survey of India: Study period: 1985-1992

Eco-cultural Zones

1. Upri Pahari
2. Majhala Pahari
3. Nichla Pahari

Places of Investigation

Total = 116
Villages = 96
Towns = 20

Distribution of Communities

Total communities = 116 (+9 after 1992)
Mean number of traits = 229.2
Total number of traits = 698

Source: Singh, 2002.

Within the state, the multivariate analysis revealed that in Himachal Pradesh most of the individual groups maintain their independent identity. But there are some major groups in the state, such as Brahman, Rajput, and Kanet, who share closer anthropometric features. On the whole, there is greater 'within-group' variability among the regional groups in Himachal Pradesh.

A significant part of data from POI project throws light on the resource use made by different communities. It clearly indicates that the ecology, resources and culture determine the resource-use, the pattern of food consumption and level of nutrition, occupation, etc. There is also an important lesson for policy makers, The developmental process, market and technology also influence the resource-use and occupations. Throughout India, the private property of land is the dominant form of ownership of resources. The nature of this ownership is predominantly by the individuals; the group ownership is negligible.

Firewood is the most important source of energy. Villages are still dependent on rainwater irrigation.

At the psychological level, it has been found that the well-to-do people have turned consumerists and their attitude towards savings is no longer conservative. This is a common observation from the apple belt of Himachal Pradesh. The economic surveys also show that, at all India level (after Punjab) the state of Himachal Pradesh has the second rank in the consumer market (Saran, 2004). But for Singh (2002), the leader of the POI project, what is most worrying is the large decline in the child sex-ratio among the higher classes. This is a negative indicator of the change in the society in the most prosperous states such as Punjab, Haryana, Himachal Pradesh, Gujarat, Uttaranchal and Maharashtra as indicated by the 2001 census (Figure 1.2).

Fig. 1.2: Decline in child sex-ratio (girls less than boys)

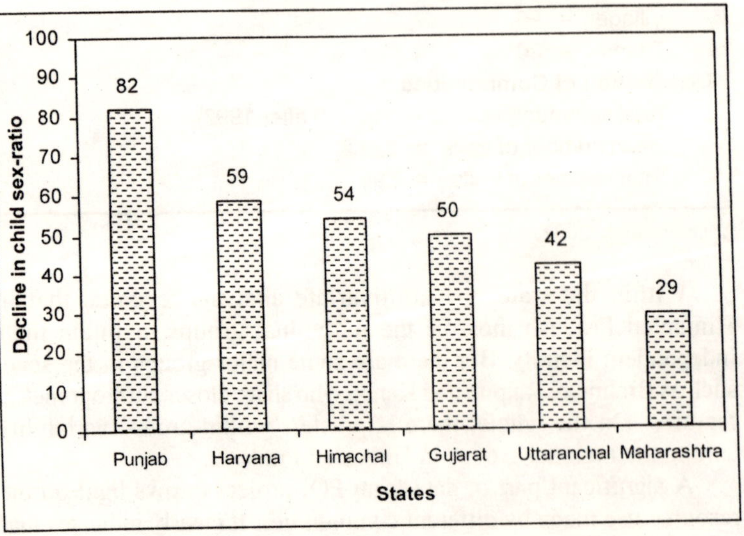

Lastly, a very positive indicator of the cohesive structure in India is the sharing of the ethos, space and traits by its people. This is a continuous process at the grassroots level. An interesting dimension of the sharing is the correlation of the traits among the various communities of India which are grouped into socio-religious categories. Keeping in view this aspect of the secular structure of the country and plurality of the beliefs among people, the last section of this volume attempts to indicate that the development of these institutions at the grassroots level is a way toward sustainability.

2

Ecology and Sustainability

We are twice born, both as biological creatures and as human beings. The former signifies our socio-biological inheritance from the apes whereas the latter emphasizes the role of socio-cultural environment in the modification of the organism. As the organism modifies itself there is accumulation of experiences in mind which are passed on to the next generation through cultural means.

It is to be noted that the process of globalisation by its very nature overlooks the local cultural complexities and advocates a universal approach. It has been often found by social scientists that the universal approach is inappropriate to understand local problems. However, above all, it is human creativity, a unique biological and cultural achievement, on which our future thrives. The cognitive uniqueness of human species, guided by science and technology, moulded in socio-cultural setting, and following the ethical and moral constraints, provides a hope for the development of all living and non-living world.

The Two World-views

All societies aspire for sustainability, which is a dynamic process. Although it has to be related to the sustenance of the life-support systems, there is a possibility of getting lost in the achievement of this goal. The present global scenario on sustainable development is divided into two camps. The dominant minority, who claim to be the managers of the planet Earth, seem to align with the selfish model of sustainable development (Figure 2.1). There appears to be a silent majority living in developed and developing countries who align with the altruistic model of sustainable development (Figure 2.2). The important characteristics of these two models are given in Table 2.1.

Fig. 2.1: Selfish model of sustainable development

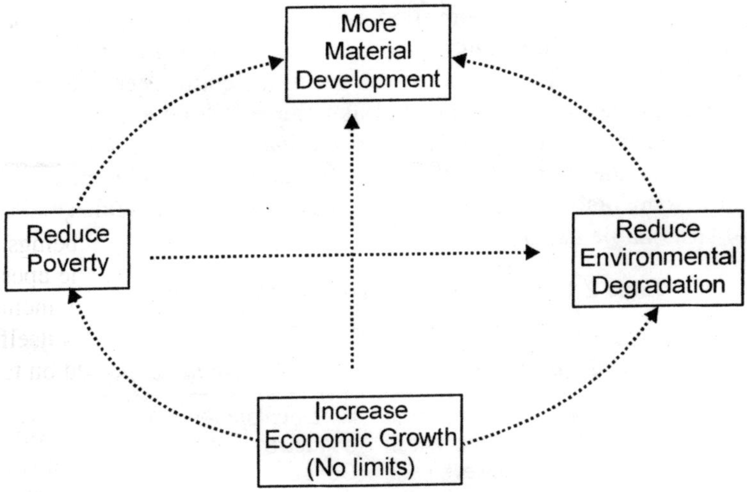

Fig. 2.2: Altruistic model of sustainable development

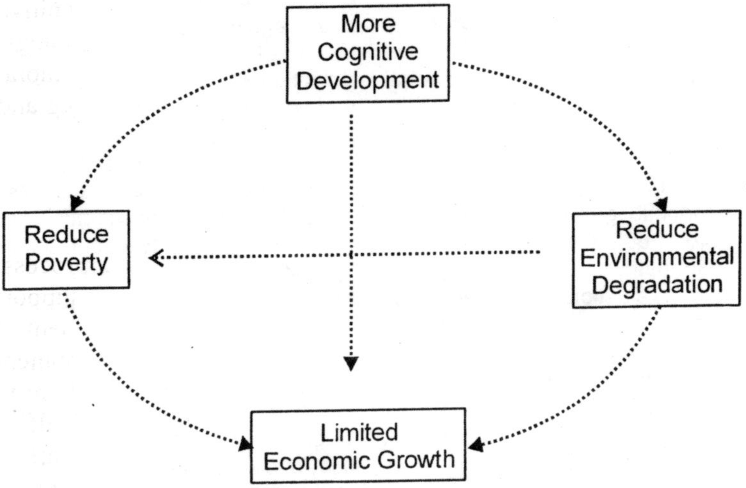

Our policies of future, at global as well as local level, aiming at the sustainable development may have to find a fine balance between these models of development. In 1997, some of the world leaders participated in a conference aimed at exploring ways of thinking about the future ranging from science to spiritualism. Then, a distinguished speaker from each of the conference sessions wrote a chapter; which were compiled in a volume on the subject of *Sustainable Development: The Challenge of Transition* (Schmandt & Ward, 2000). The views expressed in this conference, by about 500 participants, summarized in this volume fall in two contrasting groups—one *radical* and the other *incremental*. The radical view advocates the scenario as the altruistic model of development and the incremental view supports the scenario shown in the selfish model of sustainable development.

Table 2.1: Important characteristics of the two models of sustainable development

The Selfish Model	*The Altruistic Model*
A. *Development*: Identified with economic measures; Competition is main factor in achievement; contrient interdependence mainstay of society.	A. *Development*: Identified with cognitive and social measures; Cooperation is main factor in achievement; Cooperative inter-dependence essential for the society.
B. *Economic growth:* It is basic driver of development; No limits to growth; Science and technology tools to cross natural limits of economic growth.	B. *Economic growth*: Dependent upon cognitive and social factors; Limits to growth essential; Sensitive to natural eco-system and socio-psychological factors.
C. *Environmental degradation:* Caused by poor economic growth and poverty; High economic growth itself will take care of the environmental degradation; Trade regulations and valuation of resources essential.	C. *Environmental degradation:* Caused by high drive for the use of natural resources and its selfish use by few individuals and groups; Environmental degradation is the consequence of high economic growth; Ethical and social constraints necessary.
D. *Poverty:* Caused by poor economic growth; it is the absolute state of low level of energy due to insufficient material resources.	D. *Poverty:* Not associated with economic criteria; Social and psychological factors important; Cognitive factors important in alleviation of poverty.

It is important to mention that the supporters of each model of sustainable development are from developed as well as the developing world. The models do not divide the two worlds. Probably, each individual has these two tendencies, selfish and altruistic. The survival of humanity would however depend more on altruistic tendencies than on the selfish. This assumption guides the humanistic approach followed in this study.

Eugene Odum (1996), the famous ecologist, advocates a similar view in his host-parasite system visualized as the life-support model (Figure 2.3). Human beings, as prudent parasites must engage in service of the biosphere through its preservation, maintenance and repair. It is only then that humanity would get the high-quality life-support goods and services from the system. For Odum ecology is the viable link between science and the society.

Fig. 2.3: The host-parasite model

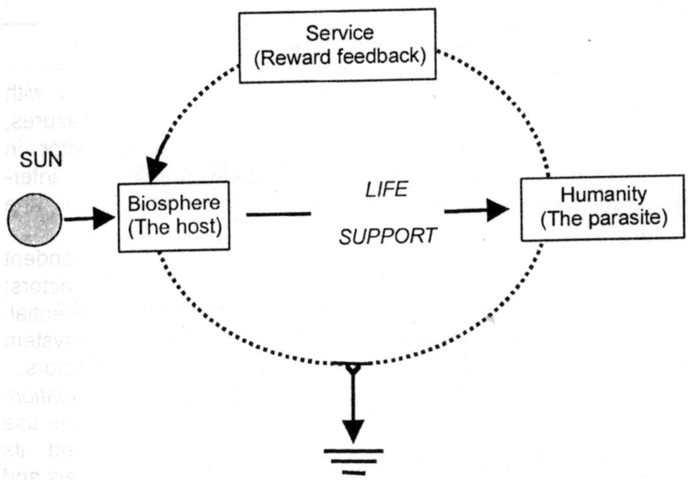

It is important to note that the predominant global view considers many dimensions of sustainable development: scientific, economic, corporate, environmental, social, religious and spiritual. It suggests the realization that the social dimension of development is important and is penetrating among the material scientists and policy makers. At least they are considering that the affected populations take leading position in the development initiatives (Schmandt & Ward, 2000). Though the reality is a far cry.

Here I would like to make a digression to socially reconstruct the scenario in my valley, about ninety kilometers from the Victorian city of Shimla, presently the capital of Himachal Pradesh. This brief social reconstruction from my memory is presented to argue the antithesis of the "poverty thesis." However, the aim is not to claim support for selfish or altruistic model of sustainable development, but to suggest certain important aspects that are often overlooked. For example, the role of observational learning in the development of appropriate behaviours; or those behaviours which are problematic to sustainable development.

The advocates of "poverty thesis" assume that the poor people degrade the environment. Let us imagine that a "poor" goes in a forest and brings back a headload of firewood for the daily needs. He may not have any other means of using the forest resources, except some fruits, honey or some other minor forest produce. He is healthy as far as biological survival is concerned. Once a "rich," owner of a logging company, visited the valley. His greedy eyes fell upon the lush green and virgin forests in the valley of Jubbal. He laughed at the local natives, the "poor" incapable of comprehending the value of those forests. The "rich" leased out the forest and started extracting timber. He had Swiss made machines to fell trees and then transported the logs over a ten thousand feet ridge with a ropeway hired from Germany. Within a few years the forests of ages were gone.

During the process some "poor" natives learned the tricks of the trade and started new way of livelihood. From subsistence farming they shifted to the trade of timber. Incentives were very high. A new process "fell the trees and earn money" began. This money brought luxury, consequently the society's values were threatened. There ensued a conflict. Partly the norms were revived and the process of "exploitation" came to an end.

Is it not the way of eradicating poverty, I reasoned, did not the "poor" learn from the "rich" the new way of behaving with the forests? Were these "poor" less intelligent earlier? The answers to these questions are important before the "poor" natives are made culprits with the charge that they are the enemies of the forests.

There is another significant question in the "poverty thesis." It makes an implicit assumption that poverty leads to the impoverishment of the cognitive abilities of people. There is no scientific evidence to support this assumption. In other words poverty may not have any negative relationship with the cognition. Therefore the advocates of "poverty thesis" have no justification in making statements such as the "poor" does not behave in responsible manner with the environment. Compare him with the "rich" having access to various components of the environment and it is not difficult to find that most of his activities create imbalance in the ecosystem.

Thus there is some logic in believing that the behaviour patterns of the "rich" indicate that he is very poor in his knowledge about the life-support system. Or, he has learned dangerous ways of interacting with the environment, which are hindrances in the path of sustainable development. On the other hand, a "poor" does not engage in these activities. Therefore he is pro-environment. However, it is difficult to understand, why developed countries want to thrust their highly consumptive lifestyle upon the developing countries (Box 2.1).

Poverty, Fertility and Environment

The issue of poverty has been analysed by Shah (1998) and Ragini Sen (2003) from the viewpoint of population growth in India using various social science perspectives, mainly theoretical and pragmatic (Chapter 4). Shah has also arrived on similar conclusions as described in the two scenarios above. His two scenarios, the ecological and economic, parallel the contrast between selfish and altruistic models. Ragini Sen (2003) seems to take a strong social psychological position to discard the propositions that characterize the selfish model (economic model) in the context of India. There is need to study the 'soft' variables to tackle the problem of population growth. She is categorical in suggesting that it is too simplistic to relate poverty with population growth; and it is not the poor who are creating the tragedy of commons.

Box 2.1: How do we define sustainability for Mohtu?

A scientist* from the Indian Institute of Remote Sensing, Dehra Dun narrates the pathetic story of the consequences of rampant mining in the trans-Giri area in Sirmaur. Mining has disturbed the vital forest-land-water-agriculture linkages. On the social consequences, a case is reproduced here.

"Having experienced eighty springs in this rugged terrain Mohtu of Dugana village (trans-Giri) considers mining to be a curse for this region. The debris rolling down the mine on the upper reaches of the

(*Contd.*)

(*Contd.*)

hill has degraded more than thirty bighas of his agricultural land. Three kulhs (small unlined water diversion channels) so plentifully constructed in this rocky terrain by his forefathers have been awaiting compensation from the mine owner, but in vain.

Glistening tears in the old and experienced eyes of Mohtu very well tell the story of rampant exploitation of the resources and the people. His ideals do not however allow him to speak out vocally, but he often breaks down into tears when describing the deteriorating social norms. Though poor, his ideals do not allow his three grown up sons to work in the mines.

The old and experienced eyes of Mohtu are overwhelmed with pain when he talks of the changing moral standards in his surroundings. Under the changed circumstances the family of Mohtu has to devote more time for firewood, fuel and water collection. Ghasnis (pasture lands) have become unsafe due to stones rolling down and flying above as a result of blasting that goes uninterrupted and unwarned. Even the approach to the fields and common lands is severely hampered due to mining induced landslides, specially during monsoons.

It is doubtful if the three children of Mohtu and their children would still prefer agriculture to mining after Mohtu is gone." (pp. 125-126)

* Lakhera, R.C. (2001). Mining and environmental degradation: Case of Sirmour District in Himachal. In M.L. Dewan, M.L. and P. Rautela (Eds.), *People's Movement for Himalayan Rejuvenation*, pp. 117-132. New Delhi: Concept Publishing Company.

The psychological and socio-economic factors related to fertility are complex and multiple. A report on wanted and unwanted fertility in various north Indian states has analysed such factors (Kulkarni & Choe, 1998). For example, they have reported that in Himachal Pradesh, Punjab, and Maharashtra, the wanted fertility was not much higher than the replacement level, but unwanted fertility was quite high. The family welfare programmes should concentrate on minimising these unwanted births. As far as education was concerned, the illiterate women in Himachal Pradesh, Punjab, and Maharashtra wanted about 2.5 children whereas the women with any formal education in these states wanted fewer than 2.3 children per woman.

It was heartening to hear the 'success story' of Himachal Pradesh in the area of primary education, "*The high level of school participation in Himachal Pradesh is entirely accounted for by the variables included in the analysis, with village characteristics (e.g. the 'village development index' and the existence of a women's association) playing a key role in explaining the differences between Himachal Pradesh and other states.*" (Dreze & Kingdon, 1999). Cohen (2000) noted, "*Himachal Pradesh may also offer a more successful example. The female-to-male ratio there rose from 884 per 1000 males in 1901 to 912 in 1951 to 976 (second only to Kerala) in 1991.*" The results of 2001 census were, however, not favourable to this thesis, it dropped to 968.

It is difficult to reason why this has happened in Himachal Pradesh where the females in the rural area have the highest ratio of economic independence (23.6%) in India. Moreover, the highest proportion of 80+ widows in India was in Himachal Pradesh (80.9%). This was a remarkable aspect of the women in Himachal Pradesh and indicated high self-empowerment (Bose, 2000). Perhaps the increase in prosperity and the access to technology of fetus sex identification may have contributed to this gender bias in drop of the child sex ratio in 2001 (Chapter 1).

It is a matter of future investigation whether the decisions to adopt such measures are to be attributed to the increasing demand for dowry (Chapter 4; Ragini Sen, 2003) or there are some other socio-psychological factors. For example, an analysis of the impact of son preference on reproductive behavior revealed that several states in northern India (particularly Himachal Pradesh and Punjab) exhibited strong effects (Mutharayappa, Choe, Arnold & Roy, 1997). Surprisingly, in every case the effect was greater for literate than for illiterate women. They have estimated that if gender preferences for children could be entirely eliminated, the level of fertility in India would fall by about 8 percent.

Amartya Sen (2001) says, "*the most disturbing aspect of this natality inequality, to wit, the "son preference" that many Indian mothers themselves seem to have. This face of gender inequality cannot, therefore, be removed, at least in the short run, by the enhancement of women's empowerment and agency, since that agency is itself an integral part of the cause of natality inequality.*" Our understanding of the folk psychology is poor and there is huge scope to improve it (Box 2.2).

Amartya Sen has also pointed out a marked sex divide in India. A recent study on gender and education throws more light on it (Mohanty

& Nandakumar, 2005). Some of the lowest sex ratio occurs in the Northern and Western sections of the country while the Southern and Eastern parts have much better ratios.

Box 2.2: Folk psychology

Kirin Narayan, an Indian-American anthropologist in her path-breaking book on oral storytelling explores the significance of folk psychology in nurturing human lives.

In 'Across the Seven Seas' Urmila explains, *"The reason that worship is performed on this day, the reason that the tree is worshipped, is so that married women will have a good married life, and those who want sons will have sons. The meaning is that the pipal tree is Brahma, the Creator.* " (Narayan, 1997; p. 32)

Kapila, a fellow at the Department of Anthropology, London School of Economics and Political Science, explores local ideals of conjugality amongst the Gaddis of Kangra. She presents examples of the complexity of relationships overlooked by the researchers.

"Marriage means several things in contemporary Meghla. Sexuality is only one aspect of marriage; care and on-going contribution to the conjugal unit are also defining features of how marriages are conceived of and lived at the present times. Shaadi (marriage) means companionship (saath), says Pratap. He and his wife Ramna have three children. If Pratap's life revolves around providing for his family, then Ramna's life pivots around making that family into a cohesive unit. Companionship, Pratap explains, is not only that of the spouse, but also of children. It ties people with the past and the future at the same time. This is because Ramna and he can become *buzurg* (old, but also in the sense of ancestors) to their future generations. Children are the most critical aspect of the family. A spouse provides you with that possibility, along with providing love and affection. Pratap makes a distinction for my benefit between *pyaar* and *muhabbat*, the former connoting love in its broadest sense, and the latter love in the romance sense. Echoing popular notions, he elaborates that the former is the more enduring one, whereas the latter is more ephemeral. Many elopements end in tragedy because those liasions fail to transform *muhabbat* into *pyaar*, he says." (Kapila, 2004)

They have suggested that the economic development has fallen short to explain it. For example, the per capita income in states like

Punjab, Haryana, Gujarat and Maharashtra is the highest and are among those having the lowest sex ratios. On the other hand, states such as Orissa, Jharkhand, and Chattisgarh, with the lowest per capita incomes, still have a equal sex ratio. Similarly the female literacy, by itself, was also not the answer. Again, states like Punjab, Himachal Pradesh, Maharashtra, and Gujarat have the best female literacy rates in the country; Orissa and Andhra Pradesh are among the worst.

In the context of western Himalaya, Prakash (1997) has made an exhaustive analysis of the relationship between poverty and environmental degradation. In the first part of his paper he analyses the central premise of the idea of a poverty trap—that there is a mutual and spiraling relationship between poverty and environmental degradation. There is however no conceptual and empirical evidence in context of western Himalayas, particularly Himachal Pradesh, to suggest that poverty has causal linkage with the environmental degradation.

Prakash has also investigated the thesis that population growth is the major contributor to environmental degradation on the grounds that it leads to increased consumption and a higher demand for natural resources. Thus it is suggested that the population growth, poverty and environmental degradation are linked. Prakash has given evidence that poverty can both enhance and restrict fertility rates depending on the impact of specific macroeconomic factors on the household. Here also, poverty acts, if at all, as an intermediate or proximate expression of other forces responsible for environmental degradation.

He reviews studies from the Himalayan region where it has been found that large scale technological intervention is the major threat to environment. Furthermore, the rural poor disproportionately pay the costs of such environmental degradation. And the distribution of benefits resulting from the use of such technologies is usually not equitable. He has sited studies that have reported little evidence that poor communities degrade their environment, rather those studies identify technology and economic factors among the primary causes of degradation (Chapter 6).

A study conducted by the Asia Pacific Socio-Economic Research Institute, New Delhi, on behalf of the Planning Commission of India, will further illustrate the preceding issue. The purpose was to assess the impact of various socio-economic development programmes in Himachal Pradesh (Anonymous, 2000). The report says that Himachal Pradesh had 28.44 per cent incidence of poverty, which is lower than the national average. Although the rural poverty at 30.34 per cent was less than the average for all other Indian States, the incidence of poverty in rural tribal areas was higher at 63.74 per cent than the all-India average of 51.94 per cent. It is emphasized that the state of Himachal Pradesh has created a new concept in socio-economic development for hill region which was viewed as a model of development by the other hill areas.

In the survey of the Solan district they found that all the seven components of the Basic Minimum Services (BMS) which formed the core of social sector programmes had presented a picture of satisfactory progress. The report highlighted the role of the non-governmental social organizations in this process. Particularly "*the third sector—RUCHI, SUTRA and PAGVS—have made important contribution in formation of self-help groups, increasing awareness about the programmes, women's rights, making Mahila Mandals self-dependent, supply of plants and imparting scientific methods of cultivation of off-season vegetables.*"

From Whole to Parts

Is sustainability a local issue that relates to the people of a small region in the Himalayas? A similar question is sometimes asked in relation to the fragmentation of States in India. For example, are smaller States better in comparison to the larger States? Perhaps smaller states can develop faster according to the aspirations of the local people. Himachal Pradesh has become a role model for the neighboring states in the Himalayan region such as Uttaranchal. But the issue is not so simple as we see it today. Firstly, the socio-political reasons during the formation of Himachal Pradesh in 1966 and in the achievement of full statehood in 1971 were not similar to the issues that were involved in the formation of Uttaranchal after more than thirty years. These socio-political issues apart, the two neighbouring States have common environmental problems but there are different minds to perceive them. The famous environmental movement, the Chipko, could evolve in Uttaranchal but not in Himachal Pradesh. But this does not mean that there was little or no environmental cognition at that time in Himachal Pradesh.

The melting of glaciers in the Himalayan region is an important issue, which would help us to look into its local and global causes and consequences. It may however affect far greater geographical area in the plains and people living there. The problem of melting glaciers also has significance from an entirely different viewpoint. That has to do with the efforts to understand the causes as to why glaciers are melting and to find out solutions to mitigate the spread of melting of glaciers either in Himachal Pradesh or in the Himalayas as a whole. There is yet another entirely different issue related to this problem. This has to do with the cognition of the factors associated with it. Those who live just close to these glaciers notice the change that the glaciers are receding and perhaps rightly attribute felling of trees as an important causal factor leading to it. But it would be difficult for them to comprehend that "global warming" may be the plausible factor associated with the melting of ice reserves all over the world including the Himalayan region (Box 2.3).

Box 2.3: Are global issues important?

There is convincing evidence now that global warming is affecting the glaciers in the Himalayan mountains. These are issues about which local people may be aware but they cannot solve the problem alone. Reduction of human interferences in atmosphere need coordinated effort from people all over the World.

It is possible to minimise human loss through local warning systems. Such short-term efforts need to be "*followed by long term intra- and inter-governmental planning involving diverse agencies responsible for conservation, construction, energy, foreign affairs, water, and tourism. They must be directed toward environmentally sound economic growth policies such as renewable energy technologies.*"*

* Mehovic, J., & Blum, J. (2004). *Global Warming and Melting Glaciers In South Asia*: Environmental, Economic, and Political Implications, SARID.

However, both at local and global level, some may quietly yield to the changes and conceptualise global warming as a natural phenomenon. Yet for some there is a human dimension associated with it that has to do with our lifestyle and thus consider the problem under human control. In the latter case, the solution lies at local as well as at the global level. In this way the approach is global but there is an emphasis to find out solutions at local level. This signifies the holistic way of living on the earth.

An alternative approach followed by some thinkers is that local populations if left undisturbed would be happier and survive well.

There are several untested propositions underlying it. The first and most important is that human populations have seldom remained isolated, they have always interacted with each other. These interactions have been spatially encompassing large segments of the globe. The second assumption that happiness is possible at smaller level is associated with the previous one. Perhaps, it is the craving for this happiness that takes people far and wide in the space.

Moreover it seems highly unlikely that even if human populations abide by some ethical code, they are not going to affect each other. The main problem that we have to underline is that we all live on the same planet. Though there can be some spatial distribution, for example land, it is not possible to divide the air we breathe, the water we use and we do not have control to restrict many kinds of organic and inorganic life support processes that we all need.

The cognitive revolution needs participation of all of us. Unless all of us endeavour to achieve this goal, the participation in resolving environmental problems will remain unequal. The methodology would also be a transitory patchwork to cover the holes in the ozone layer. There is need to emphasize that the problems may have mental origins, though they are manifested physically. But mere repetition of the age-old slogan involving human greed is not going to solve the problem.

Is it possible to reverse the evolutionary clock? The answer is no, because this hypothesis cannot be tested. The alternative question may be, is it possible to change the evolutionary process? It seems highly probable that the path of evolutionary process is changeable and the cognitive revolution is the key to it. The physical limits have little constraints on the cognitive processes. Local communities can contribute tremendously to the global processes through cognitive innovations.

If people of Himachal Pradesh remain aloof, the cost may be very high. Not only that the minds of the people will be colonized, chances of combating such colonization, in particular, and avoidance of subjugation in general, would be reduced if people of Himachal Pradesh do not participate in the cognitive revolution. However, participation in the global cognitive revolution would definitely benefit the people of Himachal Pradesh as well as the entire humanity. One such area of participation for the people of Himachal Pradesh is the global debate on the issue of the sustainability of the processes of development.

It would be an act of impropriety to say that the intelligentsia in Himachal Pradesh is unaware of these transitions at the global level. They have come out with a huge document, the *State of the Environment Report— Himachal Pradesh*, almost five years ago in 2001. This exhaustive report by the State Council for Science, Technology and Environment of Himachal Pradesh was prepared to rethink about the approaches and strategies of development with regional and global interests. The report is divided in four volumes which together include twenty-two sections.

If one continues bravely from volume one to volume four, cooling down his temper when the modesty of language is outraged, encounters intolerable repetitions and looses link while moving from one section to the other, finally he might stumble at the last section of the *State of the Environment Report— Himachal Pradesh* (22.1). A wonderful message awaits the reader and perhaps it is most appropriate for the department itself (the State Council for Science, Technology and Environment of Himachal Pradesh) that has brought out the report. It says, "*All development is related to the application of science and technology in one way or the other. The application of science and technology, in modern era, resulted in a large devastation because too much interference with nature.*" The reader would now like to pause and then close the report after reading its sermon in section 22.2, which states, "*All educational institutions should be made the institutions of traditional learning of own ancient approach to lead life in harmony with Nature. Let the syllabi be overhauled, shredding the Western concepts. Our systems are so strong that if applied in their true spirit, they will do wonders in reestablishing the ecological balance and we will be again a Nation of Golden Birds.*"

This report raises some important questions. Perhaps it would be an arrogance to think that there is something gone wrong with the intelligentsia of Himachal Pradesh? The alternative hypothesis is that the *State of the Environment Report— Himachal Pradesh* has fallen to the tragedy of commons. In this kind of tragedy, the concern is about the fate of a beautiful pasture grazed by the herds of selfish transhumants. There is yet another hypothesis to explain this behaviour. It is a radical escape from the dominant world-view. Some people might seek refuge in their golden past instead of boldly facing the situation.

Colonisation of Minds

Largely it seems that the intelligentsia have consciously chosen a path of compliance with the dominant view. There is widespread acceptance by third world intellectuals that their countries are filled up with a large population of poor, illiterate and fast breeding people. This last hypothesis has become almost a "scientific" fact for these people and needs some elaboration. Thus the main question is: do institutions of power want to induce change in the peoples' perceptions, feelings and cognitions? The fear is that this is probably the new way of colonization. Although the physical colonisation of human habitats has become obsolete, the dominant groups have now unleashed new ways of colonizing the minds of people, particularly in the underdeveloped world.

This has also led to the conflict in the minds of people in the developing countries. The two contrasting viewpoints expressed by the intellectuals in India are the glorification of the past and condemning of the present. The solutions also fall in equally opposite pathways: aping the West or aspiring for India's golden past. If there are vigorous expressions of self-grandeur there is also rampant self-accusation. For example, these assertions find ample support from two books on the environmental issues.

While making a commendable effort in synthesizing the role of the policy, the law and the judicial approach in environmental protection, Thakur (1997) has incorporated an equation [environmental impact (probably he means to say negative) = Population X Affluence X Technology] to suggest the main causes of pollution. Coming from Himachal Pradesh, Thakur seems to say (quoting "the modern environmentalists" but this may not be applicable to all) that rich person's baby is godsent and poor person's baby is pollutant. At some other point Thakur seems to agree with the claim that Indians are pollution loving people. The conflict is impeccable. How can sensible people agree with these statements? Though the author accepts that "social sensitivity" is key to environmental protection.

Finally, the author, a student of law, makes a general statement that strengthens the apprehension of the colonization of minds in the developing world. It is clear from his suggestions in the last part of the book where he writes that the environmental problems in India can be classified into two categories, *"(a) those arising as negative effects of the very process of development, and (b) those arising from conditions of poverty and under-development*." There are no takers of "*affluence and technology argument*" in the west. It has till far not been accepted in India and other developing countries. As far as the contribution of the "*poverty and under-development argument*" to environmental problems is concerned, it is an extremely complex issue. Our acceptance of poverty, backwardness and population, as the major factors of environmental problems, is most probably the expression of the influence of the colonization of mind. It is compliance to the dominant view and there is little or no verification of facts.

There is another volume coauthored by the lovers and inhabitants of the Himalayas, Dewan, a doctorate from Cornell in Soil Science and who has been Chief of FAO in various countries. The second author Routela, is also an Earth Scientist. Before we come to these two scientists, let us have a glimpse of the foreword of their volume by another inhabitant of the Himalayas, Dr. Karan Singh. Although he is an elderly parliamentarian of India, his worry was how to motivate *poverty stricken and ill-informed* individuals to protect the natural resources for their long-term benefit. But there is an important question that thinkers like Dr. Karan Singh must answer: Are poor always ill-informed and thus the root cause of environmental problems? And secondly: Are rich people always well informed and thus pro-environment in their behaviour?

As far as the two scientists, Dewan and Rautela (2001), are concerned, at page one of their volume they make their discovery public by stating that the main causes of the deterioration of the natural environment in the Himalayas were: unprecedented population growth, immigration from the plains and poverty. It is however more baffling when at page three one finds a statement that "*barring a few localized centers density of population in the region is low*." And it is followed by another statement that "*Due to lack of industrial growth the Himalayan region is faced with out-migration of able-bodied workforce*." One wonders about these self-contradictory statements of these scientists.

It is worthwhile to note that the authors lament about the loss of the age-old traditional systems of resource management. In this context they also seem to agree with some beliefs of local people of Himachal Pradesh, which by other soil scientists are considered as myths and main cause of the failures of the watershed management projects in the Shivaliks. The soil scientists, Dewan and Rautela, however, emphasise the role of these myths: "*The intricate relationship between water and the floral cover was well understood and the protected forest cover was therefore maintained on the higher reaches (the recharge zones of the natural springs) and often local deities (devatas) were installed at such places.*" (p. 60)

A naïve reader is likely to conclude that the rural people in Himachal Pradesh understand the relationship between forest cover on the hill tops and the flow of water in the natural springs. These scientists seem to agree that the recharge zones, if covered by vegetation, maintain water at the lower levels. We can leave the association of local deities and water sources for the curiosity of psychologists. The common wisdom, in the first and third statement apart, there is a big question about the nature of relationship between the forest cover and the recharging of natural springs. Let these scientists first decide and they should come with non-controversial observations supported by sound evidence.

The final blow from the colonized minds of these scientists is visible in these words: "*Almost one-half of the people living in the Himalayan mountain area live in poverty, characterized by poor health, malnutrition, chronic deprivation and shortened lives.*" (Dewan & Routela, 2001) While these scientists have no data to support these claims, they however have readymade solutions. Those solutions include: increase in production, reduction of consumption of fuelwood, revival of traditional water harvesting, family planning and so on. These scientists however do not have technology to achieve these goals, the people have to innovate it.

It is therefore difficult to draw any conclusion from the reports of these scientists and intellectuals. And there are many scientists and intellectuals who make such claims for resolution of environmental problems. It may however be instructive to frame our viewpoint about the scenario of developmental processes in Himachal Pradesh from the socio-political perspectives of the leaders of this Himalayan state (Chapter 3). Here it is important to look into the origin of the concept of sustainable development at global level.

Sustainable Development

The concept of sustainable development was made familiar by the Prime Minister of Norway in the late nineteen eighties. The Prime Minister, Gro Harlem Brundtland used her powers, as the Chairperson of the United Nations World Commission on Environment and

Development, in 1987 to induce a political will among the leaders of all nations to spread the humanistic values which harmonize with nature. Mrs. Brundtland's message had its effect in the political arena. It also influenced the scientists and social workers. For material scientists the realization of social responsibility became a major task and for the remaining it became imperative to develop a caring attitude towards the inorganic and organic elements of nature.

The follow-up by her successors and people all over the world showed a new way to come together to think about our planet for our survival and for the survival of the future generations. A significant addition was the innovation of a new index for the assessment of human development. It was Mahbub ul Haq's insight that development must have human face at its center. He was the creator of the Human Development Report published by the United Nations Development Programme (UNDP). On the basis of Mahbub ul Haq's insight and perseverance into social factors, the economist Amartya Sen innovated the Human Development Index (HDI) where the measure was to be a number which was not blind to social aspects of human lives as GNP was (Sen, 1999).

It is now clear that the foundation of the sustainable development was laid by the Brundtland report. The various dimensions of sustainable development are: economic, environmental, spiritual, religious, corporate, social, scientific and political (Schmandt & Ward, 2000). The world leaders in science, technology and other spheres of life equivocally admit that the role of ethics and leadership in shaping a sustainable society has been neglected almost globally. At the same time they also realize that the policies have largely overlooked the environmental degradation in favour of industrial growth. The managers of earth now recognize that the social dimensions of the sustainable development required the direct participation of affected people in developmental processes. It is, however, still a far dream.

In this study the society and nature are not used to define a primeval relationship between the two. Neither is our attempt here to study the relationship in historical terms; one would find it in the *Natural Premises* of Singh (1998) as far as Himachal Pradesh is concerned. The central theme of the present volume revolves around the role of socio-cognitive factors in resolving environmental issues. Since the understanding of the surrounding physical and social systems is dependent upon the cognitive and mental factors belonging to human species there are chances of subjectivity or bias in our views. The criterion to rectify this bias has to be worked out by human beings themselves. This is the biggest dilemma when we talk about the ecology and sustainability. The ecology refers to the relationship among the elements (natural and manmade) of the ecosystem whereas sustainability is the human constraint to maintain these relationships for our own survival and the survival of our future generations.

This human constraint is almost entirely defined by the human beings themselves as far as the most dominant views of environment are concerned in present times. Maurice Strong (2001), the former Secretary General of the United Nations Conference on Environment and Development (the *Earth Summit*) has presented the preceding dilemma in very simple words. He admits that, "*Even political leaders who are strongly committed to sustainable development cannot impose it upon people who do not understand or appreciate its importance. Conversely, even the most reluctant of political leaders cannot fail to pursue sustainability when their people demand it.*" Therefore the problem lies in the cognitive and mental faculties that are used to apprehend the society and the nature.

These conflicting goals, within the sectors of the state and between the center and the state, define the socio-economic terrain for sustainable development. In this scenario, it sometimes becomes utopian to talk about the valuation of ecosystem services in terms of mental peace and other psychological aspects or for example for pure air or water as the material basis of life. Our endeavour, however, is to suggest that we have to work under these conflicting situations by using our traditional base to assimilate and generate knowledge that can help in the objectives of sustainable development.

In the present essay our thrust is on the socio-cognitive approach. It incorporates people's beliefs, attitudes, perceptions and aspirations for developing an integrative vision of human-environment relationship in Himachal Pradesh, a state that has shown some uniqueness on the social indicators of the human development. In the following chapter we shall try to discern the impact of some global transitions in the developmental thinking of the leaders of this Himalayan State.

3

Water, Forest and Land

Our tradition reminds us about the scarcity of water. The *tapasya* of Raja Bhagirath in bringing river Ganga on earth is popular among the Indians. There is however another lesser-known myth. It is said that Bhagvan Sri Krishna blessed the society of Rajasthan desert that it would never face scarcity of water. With this blessing the society in the desert land did not sit idle, innovated numerous methods to conserve every drop of rain in their villages and towns. The rediscovery of these innovations by Anupam Mishra (1995) of the Gandhi Peace Foundation has been beautifully illustrated in *Rajasthan ki Rajat Boondein*. The important lesson is that the blessing of Bhagvan Sri Krishna did not make the society idle. Instead of waiting for a miracle the people took up water conservation as a sacred duty. As a result, the society that flourished in the sand covered land is famous for their brave kingdoms, business houses and magnificent art and culture.

Hypothetically, the desire to quench the thirst of the vast desert might have led to the exploration of the Himalayan rivers. Hints of such explorations for the search of water are part of mythology. One such story is associated with the natural spring at Bhagsunag up in Dhauladhars, near Dharamsala. These myths and beliefs about water are interesting part of the cognition of the people in Himachal Pradesh.

Some of these beliefs need mention here. The first one is the association of snakes with the availability of water, abundantly depicted in cultural artifacts. It is mainly associated with the apprehension of the pollution of the springs. The second is the association of vegetation cover with water conservation. The third is the perception that lakes at higher altitudes maintain water supply in the springs at lower altitudes (Box 3.1).

Box 3.1: Indigenous consciousness of water

Rinchen Zangpo [=Ratan Bhadra], a great scholar of Tibetan and Sanskrit, a renowned translator, and a tantrik once carried three water snakes in a box of rhinoceros skin, from Hopu in Kinnaur to a place Kyuvang, Guge Province in Western Tibet for the sake of water.

The belief of people about the relationship between water, snakes and the availability water is an important one (Pirta & Negi, 1996).

Nako, the last village on the Indo-Tibetan Border has population of more than 500 people. It's management system of water, which is available for few months as the snow melts in a year is unique. A canal from 13000 feet high source feeds the huge lake and and its canal system in the village.

The famous Chipko slogan reverberates in the western Himalaya: the forest and its relationship with water and air and soil, the basis of life.

क्या है जंगल के उपकार!
मिट्टि पानी और बयार।
मिट्टि पानी और बयार,
ज़िंदा रहने के आधार।

In this volume, though our objective is not to study the beliefs and perceptions of people about water, it is however important to look into these cognitive factors in the context of recent controversies about vegetation and water. It involves scientists, policy makers and common people. The aim is to sort out the problem of water scarcity and various other changes in the landscape of the Himalaya. These changes include soil erosion, vegetation loss, poverty and the developmental interventions. The main challenge is to understand the human adaptation "*to earth and biological systems that transcend the bounds of physical sciences*" (Narasimhan, 2005). One way, the scientist suggests, is to inculcate an ability to live with water on nature's terms and thus connecting the problem with the society.

Common Issues

There are scientific reports that challenge the "myths" of common folk as well as the elite class with regard to the positive relationship between vegetation and water. This issue shall be taken up in a following section. Secondly, there is an important issue where local interests have been overlooked, in favour of larger common good. For example, the creation of large water bodies by drowning the scarce land of local people and uprooting them from their native land. Third, there is thrust upon several interventions in the name of "development," where the inventions of local communities are replaced by new technology. The consequences of such changes on the society—for betterment or impoverishment—are a matter of debate.

At the same time "the altruistic love" of the developed world for the poverty-ridden people of Himachal Pradesh is a matter of concern. This issue has not received the attention of the intelligentsia who owe this responsibility on behalf of their community. It is extremely important for "the poor" people of Himachal Pradesh, who receive huge amounts of money from international organizations with packages of expertise, to mitigate their problems. These packages of expertise grossly undermine the cognition of local people including the more learned ones. However, these projects entail huge burden on the poor people in the form of loans. The public is entirely unaware of the loan being drawn from foreign institutions in the name of the noble cause of removing their poverty.

Any help rendered to "the poor" people in guise of charity may threaten the dignity of local population, lower their self-esteem and ultimately shake their confidence. These and other related issues would be highlighted in this chapter with an open mind to generate a debate where "the poor" people can have a say about their own well-being and also contribute in solving global issues.

Our approach in raising these issues follows humanist principles. It is assumed that an external group or society provides the expertise and necessary finances with the intention to help the recipient group or society. It is only the humanist approach, which believes in such voluntary altruistic principle; the modern theories of help and altruism in economics, socio-biology and social psychology do not support it. In latter sciences the principle is "you scratch my back, I will scratch yours." Therefore according to the latter group of theories, where humanist principles are missing, one must know the objective behind extending help. It is also true that in this process the costs and benefits to the helper may be economic, social and psychological. These theoretical issues are extremely important in understanding this special donor-recipient relationship.

A second issue has perhaps greater significance. Although thinking along these lines had been going on over a long period, the arguments could not create much impact. The issue is the evidence about the positive relationship between vegetation (mainly trees) and the availability of water in the springs and other natural water bodies. The native wisdom that assumes this positive relationship is elaborately described in the chapter 6 of this essay, but here we shall discuss recent researches that negate this relationship. These studies, conducted in Himachal Pradesh, and other parts of the world, state that there is a negative relationship between trees and water availability. In other words, the greater the tree-cover, the lower the availability of water in the catchments.

The third key issue is, whether the recipient social systems have become entirely obsolete and therefore need replacement by a flawless social system. This is in regard with the perceptions of the powerful donors towards the poor and helpless recipients. Not only that the donors perceive poverty of the recipients as a hurdle to "development." Furthermore, "the poor" are perceived as a burden by the rich societies and the only way to lessen this burden is through large-scale interventions in "the poor" society. The expertise provided in the management of water, forest and land exemplifies such interventions by the "civilized" rich. Its impact on "the poor" society is devastating. For example, Gadgil and Guha (1993) narrate the plight of the natives of Jaunsar, an area east of Shimla and the land of Mahasu Devta, during British Raj. When their forest rights were curtailed, they not only protested against the *wajib-ul-arz* (record of rights), but in desperation would occasionally pilferage the timber logs of the forest department.

Selfish Herd

The basic premise under technological interventions, a hidden agenda, is that unless there is market for the cognitive produce and material produce of an individual or group it will never be able to improve over the other individuals or group. For valuing its cognitive and material resources the individual or group creates need for them among the other groups in the society. The more the others feel that they need those resources, the greater is the demand for it. The net result would be the development institutions that largely protect the interests of the producers of valued items.

But the strange case is where the powerful producers assume the role of donors. These individuals or groups donate their resources to other individuals or groups even when the latter do not have means to use the donations in an efficient manner. Theoretically it is important to understand this strange altruism. Does this behaviour belong to true altruism (where the donor bears the cost of the help) or is it psuedo-altruism or biological altruism (where the donor expects benefit from the recipient)? These concerns arise from the view that poverty is both the cause and consequence of environmental deterioration. This singular discovery finds mention in large number of writings, particularly coming from dominant sources, though they provide little or no evidence to support it. It has also colonized the minds of intellectuals from those "poor" societies (Box 3.2).

However, as social scientists we have to look into this relationship objectively in the context of donors as well as recipients. Even if one assumes that poverty is intrinsic to some individuals and groups, there are several success stories, where persons from these "poor" societies have evidently achieved very high cognitive and economic standards. There are examples where individuals in the "rich" societies with very poor facilities have made path-breaking discoveries in several fields including science, but it is only later that they amass enormous infrastructure.

On the other hand it is difficult to rule out the observation that individuals or groups become richer at the cost of others. In other words, the evidence is overwhelmingly in favour of societal norms where competition is valued. The human society throughout its cultural evolution has not been able to counter the impact of the selfish gene implied in Darwin's theory of evolution. The arguments in favour of altruistic gene are not acceptable to the evolutionary scientists. In other words the altruistic gene is unable to evolve.

There are a few strands of cultural evolution that support the altruistic nature of human species. They have to bear the onslaught of the dominant egoistic drive in the current global scenario. Although metaphorically geologists talk about disappearance of some rivers, the phenomenon of "river piracy" has now become a regular feature among various states in India. The state of Himachal Pradesh in particular and the other Himalayan states in general have suffered due to this water piracy since the independence of India. The large number of displaced people from Bhakra Dam and Pong Dam in Himachal Pradesh have witnessed the consequences of such authoritarian distribution of water (Box 3.3; and Chapter 6 for related issue).

Box 3.2: Projects to remove poverty

There is no project to improve the cognitive environment where people can themselves take initiative. Rather the argument is always to remove poverty, which is worsening. A few examples are here.

Community Forestry E-News No. 2004.10

October 2004

A *Rs. 600 million ($13 million)* British Forestry plan has been launched in 90 pilot locations across Himachal Pradesh. The basic objective of the project, to be completed by 2007, is to establish a cost-effective strategy for sustainable management of forests and raise the livelihood of the poor.

World Bank funded project

Project ID: P093720 August 30 2005

Himachal Pradesh Mid-Himalayan Watershed Development Project

This *US$m.75* project would support GoHP with its plans for implementing the 2003 guidelines for *Haryali* ("greening") guidelines, which were prepared by GoI's Ministry of Rural Development and call for the active involvement of PRIs (Panchayat Raj Institutions) in the planning and implementation of watershed and economic development activities in the rural areas. For its implementation an HP 'Natural Resource Management Society' will be constituted.

World Bank funded project

Project ID: P095114; Dated November 1, 2006

US$m.400 and with local resources the SJVN will develop the Rampur hydropower project (RHPP) of 412 MW; It will use water from the tailrace of the Nathpa Jhakri power plant.

Myth and Reality

These larger inequalities in water use are extremely important but let us first take some basic issues related to our knowledge about water in our vicinity. This has to do with the relationship of water, forest and land. One of these relationships significant for us here is between vegetation and water. Further, a specific case of this relationship may be that forests contribute to water conservation in the soil. It is true that various environmentalists and others have used it in various ways. For example, the forestry people have used it to laud the value of forests.

The Myth

Let us start with an argument that the positive relationship between the forest and water is a myth. It is as follows.

"*The myth that forests act as sponges with regard to water conservation has survived in the popular media, as well as official policy in many parts of the world, even as hydrologists and ecologists have debunked its logic since the 1920s.*" (Saberwal, 1999; p. 210)

Although Saberwal has not sited standard book of hydrology or ecology in support of this strong argument, he seems to use it to treat the allergy of forest officials against the grazing herds. The argument has been recently raised by a group of scientists in the context of watershed management in Himachal Pradesh and other parts of world, to suggest that the plantation of trees in these areas may further lower the water table.

Box 3.3: Increasing the number of displaced

Dams, Rivers & People, Volume 2 (2-3-4), 2004.

The Supreme Court has directed the Himachal Pradesh and Rajasthan govts to submit the latest status reports about the allotment of land to 20,722 families rendered homeless due to Pong Dam even as they continue to strive for rehabilitation after 30 years of their displacement. The court has sought details as to how many families were yet to be allotted land in the Indira Gandhi canal area in Sriganganagar district (Raj) and how many had been given the Eligibility Certificates by the HP govt, making each family entitled to get 6.250 Ha. 1,30, 000 Ha of land was to be made available by the Rajasthan govt to the oustees as the state was the main beneficiary of the Pong Dam linking Beas with Sutlej to augment the inflow of water in the Bhakra reservoir. The petitioners, Pradesh Pong Bandh Visthapit Samiti and Himachal Pong Dam Oustees Welfare Committee, said thousands of oustees had not been given ECs even after 30 years of their uprooting and the committee appointed on the order of the court had not held any meeting since 1998. They stated that 16,100 families were issued ECs during 1974-5 but the land during this period was allotted only to 9 195 of them, leaving 6 905 families without allotments. Ironically, allotments of 6,658 families were cancelled by the Rajasthan govt during 1976-7 on the ground that they had not complied with the guidelines, fixed for acquiring the possession.

(*Contd.*)

(*Contd.*)

> The Supreme Court, Jan 28, 2004, ordered the transfer of the Pong Dam oustees' case to the Himachal Pradesh high Court for mitigation of the rehabilitation problems of 16,352 families fighting legal battle since their uprooting over three decades ago.
>
> *SPEECH BY THE THEN PRIME MINISTER AT THE FOUNDATION STONE LAYING CEREMONY, KOL HYDEL POWER PROJECT, HIMACHAL PRADESH* (SPEECH 05-Jun-2000)
>
> The then Prime Minister Shri Atal Bihari Vajpayee said, "It gives me great pleasure to be here with you today on the auspicious occasion of laying of the foundation stone for the Kol dam hydroelectric project. This is yet another milestone in Himachal's path to economic and social progress."
>
> "We have firmly placed electricity generation high on our agenda."
>
> "We do not aim at mere development, but at *sustainable development*."

Calder (2004) sums up the research of his group on this issue, "*The public perception that forests are, in all circumstances, necessarily good for the water environment, that they increase rainfall, increase runoff, regulate flows, reduce erosion, reduce floods, "sterilize" water supplies and improve water quality, has long been questioned by the scientific community. The evolving "modern" science perception suggests a more complex and generally less advantageous view of forests*." The perceptions of these scientists about the people of Himachal Pradesh are based on surveys for which they recruited some agencies. One such survey of Tiwari and Bose (2003) concludes that people in Himachal Pradesh believed that the forest cover improves water availability. Calder, the chief spokesperson of the group, is greatly concerned about these "myths" that make people plant trees, but he is not categorical about not to plant trees. It is important to mention here that as a good hydrologist he is careful in making the second statement in his summary; but his intention is not clear in making strong assertion about human beliefs and myths which also require good measurement and theory. As far as the natives of Himalayas are concerned, they show preferences for different species of trees, especially they have strongly opposed the plantation of *chir pine*, eucalyptus and poplar in the 1970s and 1980s. One reason for opposing the plantation of these species was that they lower the ground water level. May be they might have heard about Calder's research. Same is true for other associations between forest and water, it is not so simple as Calder or his survey describes, it is as "intricate" as his "modern" science. We leave this issue here and try to understand the basic argument.

Hydrological Hypothesis

First an attempt shall be made to clarify some basic concepts that scientists use in relation to water and the eco-system. The science of water is called hydrology. It deals with the occurrence, circulation and distribution of water of the earth and earth's atmosphere (Subramanya, 2005). The various components of the hydrological cycle (Figure 3.1) are important for our discussion here. The civil engineers have developed various measures of assessing these components but it is to be noted that they are interdependent variables.

Fig. 3.1: The hydrological cycle

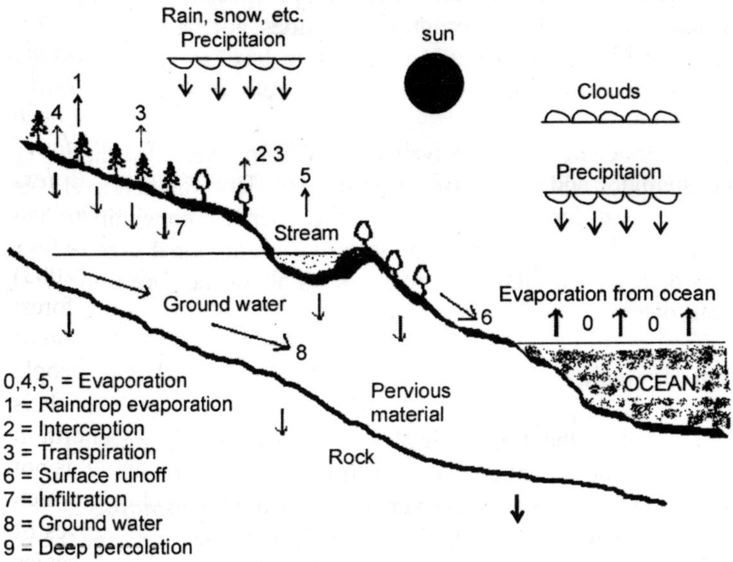

There is another important system that has acquired significance as a unit of development planning in the rural areas of Shivalik region. This is termed as the water catchment or a watershed. It is an area of land draining into a stream at a particular location. At this point the civil engineers make an assumption (probably supported by earth scientists also). They assume that the ground water divide coincides with the surface water divide or the shape and size of the catchments area. In other words the flow of water and its storage at the surface is mirrored inside the ground.

The recharge of ground water in the catchments largely depends on the structure of underground rock formations. Only aquifer store as well yield water below the surface. The replenishment of the aquifer, however, depends on infiltration of precipitation from the atmosphere in the catchments area. Therefore all surface activities, natural and human, taking place on the surface level in a catchment have their impact on the availability of water and its flow inside the ground of that catchment. These intervening variables include interception, evaporation, transpiration and finally infiltration of water. The vegetation intervenes in various ways to influence the interaction between water (inside, outside or in the atmosphere) and soil (rock). On the basis of the understanding of watersheds, it would be difficult to assume a cause and effect relationship between forest and ground water level. At least common man does not have such unitary relationship in mind when he plants a tree, to say the least he understands the positive and negative relationship of water and vegetation.

All societies have evolved ways of using water for their direct consumption and to increase the produce of plants for their livelihood. These may differ from one region to the other or even within the same region. First we shall have glimpse of the traditional uses of water and then look at other scientific views about the forest and water controversy.

Folk Wisdom

The vicinity of the shrine of Jwalaji, the area around Khundia in Kangra district, is locally called *Changar*. It is a rugged terrain of about 400 sq kms in the basin of Beas river consisting of 99 *panchayats* and 570 villages (Dewan & Rautela, 2001). In this extremely dry area the soil profile is shallow and largely the area has bare sandstone or *sappar*. The traditional structures developed by people in the Changar area for water harvesting include: *Bawari*, the main source of drinking water. There is a natural seepage within the structure. *Khatri*, it is a rain water harvesting structure. It has a small opening in the carved sand stone. The water percolates from the overlying strata. The water is generally not used for drinking. *Chappri*, small depressions in hills are used to collect water for animals and irrigation. These reservoirs are supposed to replenish water in downstream *bawaris*. *Khu*, they are wells constructed by digging the ground. They are lined with stone. But there are undeveloped wells also known as *dungali*. *Tank*, they are used for harvesting rain water, mainly for irrigation purposes. They are stone or cement lined. *Bundhs*, they are constructed at slope break in seasonal nalas for storing the rain water. It is important to mention that most of the watershed schemes funded by the international agencies include the *Changar* area of Himachal Pradesh.

Science of Water

A recent issue of the *Current Science*, a journal published by the Indian Academy of Sciences, has a photograph on its cover page (Volume 89, Number 5) to symbolize the relationship of rock, water and vegetation. This issue contains a special section on water with an objective, "*to disseminate the simple and basic facts of water on earth in general, and those specific to India in particular*." Among the eight papers, none refers to this "significant research" of the above group or to the "myths" or "beliefs" referred by this group. Four papers deal with some specific issues, whereas the other four directly or indirectly support the "myth" or "belief" of people. In his important contribution, Narasimhan from the Department of Material Science and Engineering, University of California, examines the connections between scientific knowledge and the social context of water. The attributes of water are related to life on earth. As far as *hydrological hypothesis* is concerned, it is based on the drainage networks that constitute the watershed which conveys water. Human actions can disturb it. Sediments on the flanks of the valley and stream channels are the host to variety of plant and animal communities. He did mention that desertification may affect the hydrological cycle. The two premises to meet the peoples' need of water in India— rain-water harvesting and interlinking rivers—may affect the natural hydrological cycle (Narasimhan, 2005). India has excelled in rain-water harvesting; Tamil Nadu (one-third of California) has 39,000 irrigation tanks. The impact of these structures as well as moving water on the hydrological cycle is largely not known.

In another paper, scientists from National Institute of Hydrology, Roorkee, describe the water resources of India. They have also referred to various human activities that influence the hydrological cycle, out of which there were changes that affect the water runoff and the water balance components on the basin surface. They include agricultural practices, afforestation and deforestation (Kumar, Singh & Sharma, 2005). They have suggested plant species with specific characteristics for drought prone areas or areas which are water stressed. They have not mentioned about the large scale afforestation. Rajamani (2005) from School of Environmental Sciences, JNU, New Delhi deals with the issue that concerns us here. In a brief contribution, Rajamani has visualized two scenarios, upland and lowland. In the upland scenario the trees would increase recharge and decrease discharge. As vegetation in the catchment, particularly large trees, facilitate the process of storing rainwater through extensive root zones in soils and by reducing run off as plant litters hold the water as mini check dams. Further, thicker zones of soils are formed in areas where dense vegetation cover exists. Moreover, Rajamani has a novel hypothesis that there is a strong symbiosis among groundwater storage, soil formation and vegetation cover.

Watershed Projects

Heavy investments in the watershed projects need some decision making. In lack of clear-cut scientific judgment, common sense must prevail. The selection of tree species that can thrive in less water may be a solution. There are some reports on the watershed projects that would give some idea of their achievements.

A consultant of the World Bank, Vedeld (2005) is cautious in his approach as far as the causes and possible remedies of watershed conservation and management are concerned. There is high social and natural variability in the Shivalik hills of Jammu & Kashmir, Himachal Pradesh, Punjab and Haryana where the Integrated Watershed Development Project (IWDP Hills-II with US $ m.193 for five years 1998-2004) was implemented. These strategies carried high risks. The main question has yet remained a puzzle, whether the large-scale erosion and changes in water regimes observed in the Shivaliks were mainly a result of naturally occurring high rates of erosion or expanding population of farmers and herders. The strategies in the Shivaliks needed site-specific approaches. There is also a question about the optimum density of forest. He has mentioned about some research where removal of forest did not increase erosion and there was no change in underground water table.

There are several studies in a volume edited by Iyer and Roy (2005) on these watershed projects in Shivaliks which analyse their outcome from different perspectives. Various social aspects have also been taken up. The watershed development is defined as a strategy for protecting the livelihoods of the people inhabiting the fragile ecosystem experiencing soil erosion and moisture stress. Some important social concepts are: social fencing, equitable resource use, social sustainability and voluntary participation. The watershed projects in the Shivalik foothills began with the World Bank aid in 1980 and are still continuing involving millions of dollars. The hope is that it would improve peoples' livelihoods and environmental conditions in those areas.

Forest and Society

In context of the Indian culture, the forest has its equivalent in *van* or *aranya*. This is eloquent in Tapovan by the great poet Rabindra Nath Thakur (Bahuguna, 1995). The land Bharatvarsha is known to have *aranya sanskriti* indicating that the essential element of the Indian culture has its origins amidst the forests or *aranyas*. In contrast the modern culture has its genesis in the urban or man-made centers.

This essay however follows a global viewpoint where plants and animals are important constituents of an eco-system. But in the concept of forest as it is commonly used by the Forest Department, it is not clear what kind of plants constitute the forest. Sometimes the animals are also considered as forest's secondary parts, although the plants form the main structure. Although the ecosystem approach is basic to conceptualise a forest, the policy makers, forestry people, legal experts and scientists consider forest largely as an ensemble of trees.

Here our main focus would be on the two branches of modern science associated with the plants that have been domesticated for human use. The branch that deal with plants for meeting the basic needs and for the production of surplus is the subject matter of agricultural sciences. Whereas the plants growing in the wild, partially under human control, fall in the category of silviculture, commonly known as "scientific" forestry. Their wildlife wing manages the wild animals.

There is no clear-cut definition of the kinds of plant species that constitute a forest. The same ambiguity lies in including diverse animal species as part of the forest. More recently, there has been an ongoing debate among the "managers" of forests, the elite section of the society (Prabhu, 2005) regarding some sections of human society that has lagged behind in the race of development. Should these people, the forest tribes, be denied their forest rights? They either live inside the forest or are at the edge of forest. But in either case these people are largely dependent on the forests for their survival.

In the following sections, first some more fundamental issues are pointed out having relevance to Himachal Pradesh. The main issue is the separation of "science" from the rest. This is a conscious effort by a section of society, whose aim is to dominate others by posing as experts of science. The subjugated section of the society is unable to perceive this inappropriate use of science by the experts. Besides the spread of mass subordination in the society, a side effect of this process is the development of pseudo-science, and at times formation of negative attitude towards science. However, we believe that science is the product of society.

There are several important aspects of these changes that need attention. First, the sheer neglect of historical process in understanding forest related issues. Second, misunderstanding the cause and effect relationship. Third, lack of consideration of the errors of measurement before making final judgments. Fourth, proposing alternative hypotheses and ways of testing them is an important part of scientific endeavour. Fifth, policy-making involves science as well as contribution of other disciplines. Public opinion, aspirations of people and the future of human well-being are central to policy making rather than the bare economic and scientific imperatives.

Neglect of Historical Process

In the following sections we shall look into the concept of social forestry, in particular, and the social issues associated with the concern over the forest cover of Himachal Pradesh, in general. Our aim is to evaluate some studies and prevalent policies keeping in view the five basic questions raised with regard to the claims of the experts (and assumed ignorance of the large section of the society).

There is a pioneer report by the scientists, Swarup and Chand (1987) from the agro-economic centre of H.P. University, on the evaluation of the social forestry programme in Himachal Pradesh in the early 1980s. During this period a new outlook emerged in the field of forest management in India. Some of its elements were: to develop wood-lots to arrest further deterioration of forests, to educate people what to plant and how to plant, to engage people in forest management, and to create an awareness among masses about this new "philosophy." The programme was entrusted to the forest department.

As far as the historical context of this new social stance in forest management is concerned, the two agro-economists consider the policy changes after 1950s. In the development of this social process they have entirely neglected the contribution of social workers from the Himalayas (Chapter 6) as well as some eminent scientists from other parts of India who have been directly or indirectly involved in developing the social stance in forestry. Secondly, they have also failed to notice that the process of forest denudation had been initiated much earlier by the colonial rulers and continued after the independence of India. The peasantry was not only alienated from the forestry but it had a long-lasting impact on people-forest relationship. There is excellent research by contemporary historians to support this contention (Dangwal, 2005; Guha, 1989; Singh, 1998).

Not surprisingly, when we overlook historical facts, our hypotheses are poorly formulated. The aim of social forestry according to Swarup and Chand was to alleviate rural poverty and to mobilize people towards self-reliance. They also proposed that social forestry was the "philosophy of life." The very objective thus had been far away from the achievable goals. They also made a very sensitive judgment conducive to such thinking process. At the beginning of the volume, these agronomists have made an assumption that the poor people ("50% of the population") were the main culprits who "exploit forest wealth indiscriminately."

In the same vein, they suggested a remedy for the eradication of the problem, the provision of "cheap substitutes" to the poor peasantry. Both these issues raise several scientific and ethical questions. Besides these issues, Swarup and Chand, were perhaps well aware that in 1970s and 1980s, the illicit felling of forests was rampant, particularly in the Shimla district, which involved forest personnel, civil servants and rich contractors. Consequently, as a curtailment measure, the leadership of the State was changed. This was a significant social and political event as far as the conservation of forests is concerned and an affirmative action was taken by the then Prime Minister of India. Thus, it is evident that there is a huge difference in the quantum of exploitation by the logging operations and the forest resources essential to meet the survival needs of peasantry. The two are incomparable by the humanistic criteria, the former is greed and the latter is need.

But despite this, the authors have provided no evidence to support the argument that the consumption patterns of the poor people were more destructive towards forests in comparison with the rich. The other assumption is also vague and needs a lot of research and peoples' participation. In the first instance, the agriculture and silviculture scientists should have made available to the State 'cheap substitutes.' The failure of the scientists incapacitates the State. Instead there is a general observation by all. The elite and the scientists hold the State responsible for not meeting the subsistence needs of the rural people.

Poor Research

It is an undeniable fact that the forestry is important in the economy of Himachal Pradesh and plays a significant role in the lives of the people of this hill region. This was probably more so about twenty years ago when Swarup and Chand reviewed the social forestry in the State. They reported that although 39 per cent of the geographical area was categorised as forests, the actual forest cover was only 13 per cent. One of the predictions of these investigators was that it was not within the scope of the present infrastructure in Himachal Pradesh to bring 50 per cent area under forest cover by 2000. This has come to be true. Even in 2005 the forest cover in Himachal Pradesh was 25.78 per cent but the dense forest forms only one-third of it.

In their study Swarup and Chand (1987) have proposed four hypotheses and there are a number of additional arguments. The four hypotheses are considered one by one to see the scientific evidence in their support.

The first hypothesis stated that the awareness among villagers would increase their involvement in the development programmes. The only evidence to test this hypothesis was that among the sampled non-beneficiaries, around 25 per cent households reported that they did not participate in social forestry due to ignorance about the programme. The second hypothesis was that villagers with rich resource endowment would be more willing to participate in the social forestry. Since the trees planted in the social forestry programme presumed that the family had spare land for it. Thus the evidence that there was more participation by those families who had "waste/ unproductive land" was obvious. It is to be seen whether the greater participation by the Nahan households in comparison to the Baijnath households (the two areas of study) was due to their larger land holdings or was it due to peoples' greater need for fuel wood and fodder in the Nahan area. The third hypothesis stated that programmes with local needs as well as assured and immediate benefits would stimulate people to participate in social forestry. The investigators have hardly any data to test this hypothesis. The fourth hypothesis was that the appropriate environment motivated people to participate in social forestry. Like the third hypothesis, this hypothesis was also accepted without relevant data.

In science the hypotheses are accepted or rejected on the basis of data and its analysis using appropriate tests. These scientists neither had appropriate data nor did they use any test to verify the hypotheses. Thus the hypotheses, which were proposed to make the report "scientific," were merely based on the anecdotal records. In this way, though the review by Swarup and Chand makes an important contribution by highlighting the social aspects of forest management the various points raised by them need more information. Only then will the policy makers realize the importance of the social factors in the management of the forests. These scientists were not optimistic about the prospects of the social forestry programme being run by the forest department. Unless there are alternative ways, it is important to support the existing institutions.

There are grave misconceptions in the minds of materialists in general and some biologists in particular that the social factors were simple and even easier to manipulate, It was rather the complexity of social interactions and relationships that have baffled scientists who had often taken recourse to simpler models among animals or by making simpler assumptions about the social phenomena that they intend to study.

A botanist from Oregon, Zobel (1987) measured stress in the Himalayan ecosystems through the leaves of plants. Without giving any convincing definition of "stress" in the ecosystem, which he claimed to have measured, the scientist jumped to suggest the ways of reducing this stress. His suggestion was: reduce human and livestock growth; and, develop sociologically acceptable methods for limiting the harvest to sustainable yield. Had those methods been known to science, the humanity would not have suffered. However we appreciate the concern of these scientists towards the Himalayas and its people.

Even more interesting is the case of the scientists belonging to the Himalayan region. For these scientists, the tribal and other backward castes become the scapegoat for all wrong that has been going on in the Himalayas. For example, Mehta and Sharma (1987), agriculture scientists from Palampur, claim to have measured the energy required by each individual on daily basis (least bothering about the measurement error) by collecting anecdotal records of production and consumption in the households of the tribal population of Pangi in Chamba district. These scientists concluded that the modern technology increased the energy production from agriculture farm. Therefore the betterment of the tribal population was related to the adequate technological know how.

The botanists from the adjacent State, Uttaranchal, Paliwal and Singh (1987) did not even care for providing the accurate data on the forest cover in the Himalayas. They wrote, "The forests which cover nearly 60 per cent of the land are the main glory of the Himalaya." But this glory was threatened due to the nomadic Gujars. The charges against these nomadic herders by Paliwal and Singh were: (*a*) "They dwell in forests and alpine areas throughout the year." But these people are nomadic and migrate up and down the hills and mountains. (*b*) They have huge herds of cattle "for their own needs." Gujjars however sell milk, butter and other dairy products in the market and thus serve the society. (*c*) They "indiscriminately damage the vegetation." It is not true. (*d*) They have created "barren patches in the forests." There is no evidence for it. On the other hand there is enormous evidence that the interventions by the experts in agriculture and silviculture have created brown hills in the Himalayas.

In the same volume, in which the preceding three studies have been reported, there are two more studies by the scientists from Himachal Pradesh University. The first study is by the botanists Singh et al (1987) which pertains to the morphometric analysis of the Renuka Lake in Sirmour district. Although the contents are not relevant to this section, some observations on the scientific methodology are instructive. These botanists seem to provide a "theory" of the origin of the Renuka Lake which was related to the geological changes in that area. They had neither referred to any geological source nor did they site any expertise in geology. Moreover the observations were narrated in the text in such a manner as though they were witness to the event. They have entirely ignored socio-religious aspects attached to the formation of the Renuka Lake, materially, socially and cognitively.

The other study is by an economist, Guleria (1987), on the management of cold arid desert in Spiti. The Desert Development Programme in the Spiti, a tribal belt of Himachal Pradesh, was carried out in two phases: 1977 to 1981 (with Rs.46 million input) and 1980 to 1985 (with Rs. 43 million input). This programme involved: silvopastoral development and social forestry; watershed approach; individual beneficiary activities and human development, research and training. It was felt after evaluation of these programmes that the involvement of peoples' organizations was essential in planning, formulation and implementation. This observation is frequently reported in the evaluation of such programmes but every new programme is made in isolation from the larger sections of the society. The latter only knows about it when the political leader makes an announcement. Are we not learning these lessons by paying exorbitant costs?

The other basic question that needs to be addressed, while taking up these programmes, such as the Desert Development Programme in the Spiti which involved huge amount of money, is to understand: (*a*) the causes of desertification, and (*b*) the strategies to arrest the process of desertification. It was assumed while preparing these projects that the causes of desertification were fully understood and the strategies involved were well tested. It however, appeared that the scientific knowledge on both these aspects was lacking. In his note on drought, development and desertification, an experienced civil service officer having a long experience in handling environmental issues in India, Jayal (1987) observed that, "*Like all major ecological problems, a systematic understanding of drought and desertification is difficult.*" He warned that the interventions suggested through agricultural practices (including silvopastoral practices) have largely ignored science. These interventions may lead to man-made scarcity of moisture in the arid zones and thus further complicate the problem of desertification.

For example, some soil scientists (Gupta & Joshi, 1987) were confident that the two major impacts of deforestation were soil erosion and depletion of water table. Consequently there could be drying up of springs and eventual desertification of the region. The observations of these Earth Scientists from IIT Roorkee are in stark contrast to the recent findings of scientists from IIT Delhi and others from the UK. All these studies pertain to the Himalayas and particularly to the Himachal Pradesh. These recent studies have questioned the wisdom of the local people of Himachal Pradesh as well as the scientific evidence of the experts.

To summarize, the relationship between the forest cover in the hills and its relationship with the availability of water in springs and below the surface is not necessarily positive. These scientists reported that planting trees in the catchment area might in fact reduce the water in the springs and aquifers. They have therefore warned that the large scale afforestation programmes in the Shivalik region of Himachal Pradesh and other states needed re-evaluation. Thus any policy decision may now have to consider these research finding reported by the scientists from the civil engineering departments of the prestigious institutions in India and UK.

Controversial Policy

In addition to the above controversy, raised by experts about the negative relationship between vegetation and water, a group of social activists is also on the warpath with the forests in Himachal Pradesh. Some of these social activists are engaged in environmental awareness campaigns, protection of forests and the literacy drive in the State. They have done commendable work in these areas. But it is difficult to understand the U-turn they have taken in the recent past. In their new campaign, some of the demands are perhaps related simply to the controversial statistics of the area under forest cover in Himachal Pradesh.

A part of this controversy arises from the fact that there is no clear-cut definition of the forest. The recent forest surveys using modern methods of measurement, the interpretation of satellite imageries, categorize the forest cover according to the crown density ("Dense forest"—crown density above 40 per cent; "Open forest"—crown density 10-40 per cent; and, "Scrub forest"—crown density below 10 per cent). Following this categorisation, the Forest Survey of India in 2003 reported the total tree cover in Himachal Pradesh as 25.78 per cent, out of which the Open Forest was 16.12 per cent and the Dense Forest was 9.66 per cent.

The other factor of controversy is the undestanding that 67 per cent geographical area of Himachal Pradesh is under the management of Forest Department. This is also known as the legally defined forest area. Most of this area does not have any tree cover and is not suitable for agriculture.

The third and most significant part of the controversy is the variety of tree species that constitute the tree cover in the Open forest and Dense forest categories. Some species of trees, such as eucalyptus, poplar and *chir-pine* are not considered good for wildlife and for the conservation of water. Therefore the utilitarian aspects of the trees, natural as well as planted constituting the forest, needs consideration.

The group of social activists under the convenorship of Kulbhushan Upmanyu has formed a platform to address natural resource manangement issues in the context of the Himalayas. The secretariat is presently located at Palampur in Himachal Pradesh. This organization, *Navrachna*, was constituted in 1994, "*through the support of the International Centre for Integrated Mountain Development* (*ICIMOD*)." It is important to note that though this social forum idealises self-reliance and self-governance, the activities, meetings and conferences are financially supported by a larger international organization. Therefore the independence of such social forums remain doubtful.

Some of their policy recommendations are given in a document (available from the website: www.navrachna.org), "*Parvatiya Vikas ke liye Rashtriya Himalaya Niti* (National Himalayan Policy for Mountain Development)" prepared in January 2005. This document gives a brief socio-political background of mountain development, recounts the contributions of the Himalaya, adopts the ICIMODS's ideas of mountain specificities and stress, emphasizes sustainable development approach, and suggests policy areas and interventions for the development in the mountains.

Social forum's approach for sustainable development needs mention here. One of the thrust areas of the social forum is the livelihood based conservation approach. In order to achieve it they have given an extremely calculative but controversial solution. They demand the redistribution of the forested area to increase the land holdings of the poor peasantry.

The social forum argues that, "*In Himachal Pradesh, for example, there is only 10.5* per cent *land area under agricultural cultivation against 85* per cent *in Punjab. Meanwhile, HP has 67* per cent *forest area as against 8* per cent *in Punjab. It is evident from the above statistics that without using the forest land for sustainable livelihoods, it is just not possible for any government or society as a whole to sustain the human population of the Himalayan region in a dignified manner.*" In order to achieve this goal they are asking the government of Himachal Pradesh to redistribute its 67 per cent forest area by allotting almost half of it for the sustainable livelihoods of people.

The forum's objective is laudable but the assumption that the State has 67 per cent area under forests is an extremely politically motivated statement. It does not have any scientific basis since the Dense Forest cover in Himachal Pradesh is only 9.66 per cent. The convener of the forum and its members are apparently not so innocent to be unaware of this fact. Furthermore, about 20 per cent of the area classified as the forest is inaccessible and therefore not suitable for agriculture or forestry. Therefore the forum seems to suggest that the Dense Forest and the Open Forest be put under the livelihood forestry.

The dangerous implication of the social forum's demand would be an additional pressure to lift the moratorium on the felling of trees in the Himalayas. Some agencies, with vested interests, were already active in the State. There were also reports that farmers have already encroached considerable portions of the forests in various areas. It is also reported that farmers were motivated to plant only those trees providing immediate and sizeable return, such as the eucalyptus, poplar and *chir-pine* (Swarup and Chand, 1987). The members of the social forum however strongly oppose the plantation of these tree species. In this way there are a number of controversial issues that the social forum must resolve before making a strong plea for the redistribution of the already scarce forest area in Himachal Pradesh.

If the social forum insists on the scientifically inaccurate figure of 67 per cent area under forest, in all probability their good intentions would be interpreted as politically motivated serving the interests of few vested parties while harming the interests of the larger farming community of the state.

Basic Issue

Why has there been lukewarm response from the forestry, planners and politicians to share forest control with panchayats? Academicians are, however, uninvited guests in healing the wounded relationship between the people and their forests. There has been laudable attempt to disseminate information on *Chipko*, *Sukhomajri* and *Ralegaon Shindi* (Guha, 1999; Sarin, 1996; Gadgil & Guha, 1995). Another significant aspect of contemporary writing is that specialists have converged to consolidate the association of the people with their forests. The negative attitude of the Forest Department in assimilating this indigenous expertise and information is clear from their preference for the outdated silviculture practices that never had an ecological basis. A country with third largest scientific personnel pool is unable to map out its biological resource potential, except sporadically for timber. From the silviculture age we have yet to usher in to biodiversity age.

A country that has the basic community structure to preserve the village forests and sacred groves sends its forest officers to England to learn about social forestry. The village Van Panchayats of Uttarakhand and the Village Cooperative Forest Societies of Kangra in Himachal hold great promise to involve villagers in forest conservation and management (Singh & Ballabh, 1996). A considerable spade work in this direction has already been done by the scientists at Center for Ecological Science at the Indian Institute of Sciences, Bangalore involving NGOs from all over the country (Gadgil & Rao, 1998). They envisage national level and state level institutions to achieve this objective starting from the Village Nature, Health and Education Committee (VNHEC). The basic premise is that *gram sabha*, the village council, is the owner of all natural resources, especially the biological diversity resources.

India needs to assimilate Nehruvian and Gandhian vision of development to find out a middle path. In this endeavour of formulating the middle path, we cannot overlook the social inequalities gaping at us. Our action must be to remove these social inequalities. In this context A.P.J. Abdul Kalam quotes Amartya Sen that the central issue is to expand the social opportunities to people (Abdul Kalam & Rajan, 1998).

From a nomadic Gujar to transhumant Kinnaura or Gaddi to a modern orchardist, the forest is intricately connected with the survival of people in Himachal. Any policy decision counterproductive to the availability of social opportunities to people is a threat to the congenial social, political and economic life of a State. Gender issue is also important. In this context, Cranny (2001) concluded that, "*One of the most observable impacts of development on the lives of women is the deterioration of the forests, caused by clear cutting for plantations.*" She further observed that women in the villages felt less positive impact of social forestry projects.

Future Scenarios

Some current studies indicate improvements in scientific methodology in various areas related to the forests and wildlife.

1. *Dissemination of information*: Some elementary information is now easily available on the various websites. For example, from "Great Himalayan National Park.htm" we find about its area, animal and plant species, and ecological zoning. An interesting feature is that forestry people are now conscious of their relationship with local people and their livelihoods. On the same lines the Forest Department is disseminating information related to community forestry (*Sanjhi Van Yojana*—2001). This is an important mile stone and will go a long way to change the perception of people. The Forest Sector Review is a good exercise and invites suggestions from people.
2. *Forest area*: Using a phenologically-dependent methodology the forest cover of Himachal Pradesh was estimated (Joshi, Singh, Agarwal & Roy, 2001). The area covered by forest was 17.15 per cent, whereas the forest cover reported by the Forest Survey of India was 22.5 per cent of the total geographical area of the state. The differences were attributed to small patches of tree farmlands, which could not be mapped as non-forest by FSI or the alpine scrub which also could not be categorized separately.
3. *Agriculture*: For sustainable agricultural planning there is great need of agro ecological zonation, which picks up homogeneous units of land on the basis of important parameters for specific crops in the State. These maps include many biophysical parameters: physiographic variables, climate, soils, land cover, and productivity. They are combined with decision rules (Immerzeel, Pradhan, & Bhagat, 2004). About 107 zones are available for decision makers in Himachal. Using a software one can find out where apple can be grown in Himachal. FAO has databases for 1,700 crops that can be used for this pupose.
4. *Medicines*: Misra (2003) has collected useful base line information on medicinal plants conservation and sustainable utilization from various states of India including Himachal

Pradesh. In its diverse physio-geography the state is very rich in medicinal plants. There was a need to improve policy and institutional back up for this sector. In this survey it was noticed that some local health traditions were practiced; though they were in decline. There is possibility of linking local livelihoods to medicinal plants.

5. *Transhumance*: Do transhumant systems differ from sedentary ones in their impact on the pastoral environment? According to studies by FAO, transhumant systems are potentially less damaging than sedentary systems because they exploit the herbage at fixed seasons, often at the peak of its production, and leave the vegetation to recover for the remainder of the growing season. Some conclusions from the Himalayan studies are: Overuse of pastures, forage production is low, seasonal feed shortages, changes are occurring — e.g. reduction in herd size — and pastoralists are becoming sedentary, and uncertainty about the grazing rights. Bimal (2003) reported that transhumant stock rearing was very common throughout the Himalayas. There are various nomadic groups, such as Gujjars, Kinnauras and Gaddis, who keep sheep, goats and even buffaloes under such systems in Himachal Pradesh.

   There were about 2.1 million cattle, 7,00,000 buffaloes, 1.1 million sheep, 1.1 million goats and 14,000 horses in the State about five years ago. The scarcity of fodder and erosion of traditional ethos among people is leading to the problem of stray cattle.

   The stance taken by some environmentalists and forest officials is of alarmist nature and has been discussed by Saberwal (1999) in study of Gaddi pastoralists in Himachal Pradesh. His analysis seems more tilted toward presenting the problem in the global context, it has less to do with solving the problem of Gaddi shepherds and those faced by the forest officials in the state. It undermines both these actors in the solution of problems and thus there is enough scope for the third, the elite academician, who comes once a while to visit them. The Gaddis and their way of life (Verma, 1996) are almost forgotten in such debates, these populations become pawns in the game and their destiny is written by few decision makers.

6. *Wildlife*: This area is utterly neglected. In comparison to Western Ghats in the South, the wildlife enthusiasm in the society in northwest Himalayas is almost nonexistent. A good attempt was the preparation of directory of national parks and sanctuaries in Himachal Pradesh by Singh, Kothari and Pandey (1990; Appendix 3). There is enormous scope to acquire information on flora and fauna in each of these protected areas. Investigators, sometimes draw hypothetical conclusions about the population growth, extensive farming and biodiversity. There is a need to conduct surveys about the population of animal species, knowledge of their food habbits is important (Appendix 4). Other aspects are the study on hunting of large mammals an ' pheasants in Himachal Pradesh and adjacent regions. Only 8-10 per cent of people in a village hunted, but others shared the meat obtained by them (Kaul, Hilaluddin, Jandrotia & Gowan, 2004). In Himachal Pradesh widely hunted species were cheer pheasant, chukor, koklass, Himalayan monal, western tragopan, barking deer, goral, Himalayan black bear, Himalayan brown bear, Himalayan tahr, musk deer and leaopard. It was however a sparetime activity. More deeper studies are needed to understand the human-animal relationship in Himachal Pradesh.
7. *Biodiversity*: The biologists in the universities and in the colleges collect huge information on the taxonomy of plants and animals. Largely, this work remains in isolated research papers and theses in libraries. There is a need to monitor this work through a central agency and compile it in a simple fashion for dissemination among the interested people. The biodiversity registers at local level should be the objective of such endeavours where people also participate in this global work and contribute their experiences (Gadgil, 2001). For example, there is an interesting case of the accidental spread of silver carp in the Gobindsagar, it has ecological significance as well as huge benefit for human beings (Box 3.4).

New techniques for measuring the diversity of vegetation in particular landscapes are evolving. The Indian Institute of Remote Sensing has developed geospatial model to map the biological richness of a landscape (Chandrashekhar, Singh & Roy, 2003). The forests of Himachal Pradesh were rich in biodiversity. The mixed coniferous forests were not only rich in diversity (8.15 with 440 species) but had high Total Importance Value (TIV= a measure of economic value of various plants). Where the human disturbance was high the biological richness was low and vice versa. These methods are quick and the error can be estimated. Their estimate of forest in Himachal Pradesh is 24.93 per cent of the total geographical area. According to them the orchards constituted 542.77 km^2 (0.97 per cent of total area) and agriculture was done in 7924.46 km^2 (14.2 per cent of the total area).

Box 3.4: Silver carps in Gobindsagar

The silver carp, *Hypophthalmichthys molitrix* got an accidental entry in Gobindsagar in 1971, when 47 specimens in the size range were washed out into the reservoir from the nearby Deoli fish farm. Although stray individuals and a few juveniles were reported in the landings in 1974, a significant appearance of the species in the fishery was noticed only since October 1977, when a number of juveniles appeared in the commercial landings. During 1977-78, 10 t of silver carp, were captured, which accounted for 1.4 per cent of the total landings. In the subsequent years, the fish contributed up to 72 per cent to the total catch. Its population increase had also aided in an unprecedented rise in the fish yield from the reservoir.

In view of the wide feeding spectrum and high fecundity of the silver carp, the species appears to have ecological advantage over the other species. The fish has extended through all zones of reservoir with stable winter and spring fisheries, whereas the fishing grounds of Indian major carps are location-specific. While 90 per cent of the *catla* catch is harvested during the monsoon season, silver carp supports a steady fishery throughout the year, thereby apparently making it more lucrative from economic angle. However, the role of silver carp in the fisheries development of Indian reservoirs in general and the Gobindsagar in particular is a subject of animated controversy.

Ecologists fear that the exotic carp, by virtue of its common food niche threatens the indigenous catla. Despite its gaining entry in a number of Indian reservoirs located at varying geoclimatic regions of the upper peninsula, Deccan plateau and the southern tip of the sub-continent, silver carp is not naturalised in any of them. Only in the cold water regime of Gobindsagar, where the fish was exposed to an environment akin to its original habitat, it commenced successful breeding and proliferation.

Source: Sugunan, V.V. (1995). *Reservoir Fisheries of India*. FAO Fisheries Technical Paper, No. 345. Rome.

The Polity and its Dilemma

The following words of the first Chief Minister of Himachal Pradesh, Dr. Y.S. Parmar, seems most appropriate in summarizing the views described above. This visionary man placed Himachal Pradesh on the sound footing. It is now for the people of the State to realize his lofty ideals. Parmar gave a glimpse of his vision of sustainable development while speaking in the magnificent conference hall of the Forest Research Institute at Dehra Dun as early as 1977.

He said, "*Total environment is the outside dimension in the planned development harmonizing the internal dimensions of socio-economic considerations coupled with sound ecological thinking. Through this alone the eco-system can be planned and programmed to achieve optimum productivity. I am quite clear that we have to continue to develop, notwithstanding the absence of adequate data on soils, vegetation and climate and ecological directions in the western Himalayas, just as the more highly developed countries did in their earlier years of development but as we move forward we must not feel complacent about our research and analyse and integrate the findings within our programme to achieve higher level of stable productivity as we go along.*" (Parmar, 1985)

Although the policies of the State (the Government of Himachal Pradesh) are constrained by the directions coming from the Centre (the Government of India), the leaders in Himachal Pradesh who succeeded Dr. Y.S. Parmar, have successfully kept a fine balance between the two. The political leadership in Himachal Pradesh has always identified with the grassroots people who are largely dependent on the natural ecosystem. There are instances (e.g. raising the issues of local people's rights over land, water and forest) when the leaders of the State favoured policies which benefited the ecosystem people at the cost of annoying the planners at the Centre.

In 2002, Prof. Prem Kumar Dhumal, the Ex Chief Minister of Himachal Pradesh affirmed his concern over the question of Centre-State relationships with reference to the issue of decentralization. His opinion in the meeting of the National Development Council was, "*As for earmarking the outlays for various programmes out of the pool of central assistance, it is felt that all such earmarking should be done away with and the central assistance allocated to the States as untied so that they could determine their own developmental priorities.*"

Conceivably a leader with the longest experience in the political scenario of Himachal Pradesh, Shri Virbhadra Singh, argued in front of the 12th Finance Commission of India with a firm determination that, "*We must appreciate that in a federal set up such as ours, many a times, financial consideration must be subordinated to political needs and aspirations of people*." He further added that in the face of constraints, the State has always focused on "*people-centric*" developmental policies. The efforts of these policies are now perceptible in various indices of human development such as high literacy, improved health status, better provision of drinking water, almost complete electrification in the rural areas and above all the maintenance of peace in the State.

The policies of the State government are in a dilemma. For example, in the forestry sector the emphasis is to empower the local communities and make them stakeholders in the management of forests. But at the same time this goal is being achieved at the cost of huge financial borrowings from the World Bank and other agencies. There are alternative solutions also (Box 3.5).

We need to ask some basic questions from ourselves. Although it is advisable to hire expertise in the area of advanced technology, a similar trend in the empowerment of peasant communities is worrying. Are our universities in the State or in the country incompetent to produce management personnel or social scientists who can understand the problems of the village households? We find that the research and consultation work in the '*participatory forest management*' is not assigned to local agencies. On the other hand it is true that the outside agencies use the local personnel to collect the requisite information.

Box 3.5: Corporate social responsibility

Madhav Mehra in 2005 writes:

"Ever since its inception, the World Council for Corporate Governance has claimed that corporate governance is not just about disclosures and compliance but a powerful engine for social and economic transformation. We believe that its five pillars, transparency, equity, accountability, participation and corporate social responsibility, on which the edifice of corporate governance stands, are the key to sustainable wealth creation because they allow the markets to function effectively. Markets are also reshaping the social agenda for business.

(*Contd.*)

(*Contd.*)

Business has been the greatest beneficiary of globalisation. For the first time in human history business has the power and the technology to make a difference in human lives. It is in the vested interest of business to ensure that the poor are included in the market economy and income disparities are abridged."

Mr. Madhav Mehra is the President of the World Environment Foundation and has several important suggestions (Mehra, 2005).

- Hunger is more an issue of delivery than donation. Total expenditure required for elimination of starvation and nutrition is $19 billion. Compare it with US military budget of $416 billion.
- The experience has shown that the problem of poverty cannot be solved simply through handouts. No amount of handouts can help an African farmer whose milk is unable to compete with the western farmer simply because the cows of the western farmer are subsidized at the rate of $2 per cow per day which is twice as much as he makes in the whole day.
- Handouts suffer from lack of transparency, accountability and efficiency in the delivery system. The problem is not only with disbursing governments but also with lending agencies and funding organizations. Funding organizations have little regard for the virtues of transparency and accountability when applied to themselves.
- Actually, the poor do not need handouts. They need healthcare, education and infrastructure. Infrastructure plays a far more important role than most people imagine in the development process. Developing rural markets by encouraging transparency in governance structures will unlock the hidden assets of rural poor and accelerate their integration in the market economy.
- *Knowledge is the measure of wealth in today's economy.*

It is a matter of scientific query that many of the tools used by the social scientists from outside agencies are not standardized on the particular communities on whom the project is being implemented. Mostly the data is gathered through questionnaires; the reliability and validity of these tools is unknown. Though the schemes are yet to be implemented on the local population, their participation is not elicited at the stage of project formulation. Besides, the project is time bound and the money is to be spent on certain budget heads, and there may be little flexibility to divert or withdraw from the scheme.

It is significant to note that the outcome of the watershed projects, that are implemented in several western Himalayan states including Himachal Pradesh, is being debated even in the British Parliament and have made headlines in the International newspapers. However, there has been no public/scientific debate in the State. Furthermore, some scientists conducting research on the watershed schemes, in various parts of the world including Himachal Pradesh, have suggested that by planting trees under these giant schemes the money is being wasted (Box 3.6).

In 2004, a workshop on "*Towards attaining Environmentally Sustainable Water Policy for Himachal Pradesh*" was organized by the Himachal Pradesh State Council for Science Technology and Environment in collaboration with the Indian Institute of Technology, Delhi, Centre for Land Use and Water Resource Research, University of New Castle, U.K., and the Department for International Development (DFID) U.K. However no such issue was brought to the notice of public of Himachal Pradesh where the trees have negative relationship with water, or in other words the plantation of trees may reduce the water level in the soil. People in Himachal Pradesh, the research of these scientists show, have myths about the forests that they bring rain or increase underground water level. These myths were reported not only among the rural population but even among the Himachal Government officials. It is strange that the agencies financing and coordinating these projects are engaged in the contradictory propaganda.

Box 3.6: New ways of colonization!

"*How a watershed project stopped mountains walking*"

(World Bank *India—Newsletter* Vol. 3 No. 4, January 2005)

This catchy phrase sums up the achievements of World Bank's project on watershed management in the Shivalik hills of north India. Earlier such projects involved little or no community participation, but now they claim that the driving force is the Participatory Rural Appraisal (PRA). PRA "*is a set of techniques to involve local people in planning, implementation, and evaluation of development projects.*" (Roy & Iyer, 2005) The World Bank also reports some perceptible changes seen

(*Contd.*)

(*Contd.*)

through the eyes of the local village *pradhan* "*The project has shown us light*." The water level in the watershed area also increased.

The expert power was challenged!

"Millions 'wasted' planting trees that reduce water"

shrieks the Telegraph of July 29, 2005

All the above-mentioned claims of the World Bank funded projects have become a matter of controversy now. The newspapers all over the world carried more or less similar story of a scientific research on the watersheds, not surprisingly these projects were also funded by the same agency.

The *Select Committee on Science and Technology* of the *United Kingdom Parliament* also inquired about the research by the Centre for Land Use and Water Resources Research, University of Newcastle upon Tyne (CLUWRR). CLUWRR has carried out land and water related research in all regions of the world for DFID, World Bank, FAO and other development organisations. They have found that the relationship between forest and water is based on myths not on science and therefore many watershed management projects need re-evaluation. One of the scientists, Ian Calder with Ashvin Gosain (IIT, Delhi) revealed that increased tree planting in Indian states of Himachal Pradesh and Madhya Pradesh has had a negative effect on water supplies (16 per cent to 26 per cent reduction in water yields).

The blame for all this has fallen upon the common wisdom of the "poor" people of Himachal Pradesh and those in the other parts of India—they cherish the "myth" about the positive relationship of forest and water. The problem does not end here, the Centre and the State borrow more and more money, without responsible decisions about its return, to remove poverty. For example, at the centre the interest payments alone amounted for 50 percent of the total government revenues (Chandra Mohan, 2003) and in Himachal Pradesh the per capita debt was Rs.16,000 in 2001. The fear is that this is a new way of colonization.

The government of Himachal Pradesh has the distinction of evolving policies that are oriented to strengthen the village level institutions. It is also true that it cannot hide its dream of industrialization. This is in stark contrast to the nature of the human resource it has, which is agrarian. Even if the State government chooses the path of ushering in the area of horticulture, it is hard to compete in the open market without giving subsidies to the peasants. There is another dream, to harness its rivers for hydropower (Box 3.7). But it does not have the resources, however the hydroelectric schemes implemented by the center is increasing the miseries of the people by displacing them from the river valleys. The central government wants Himachal Pradesh to generate its own financial resources by felling green trees.

Box 3.7: New life or a death trap

From *Khab*, the point where Sutlej enters Indian territory, to Gobindsagar, the Sutlej valley is under intensive technological intervention, for generation of hydroelectric power. The last intervention has been proposed at Khab to construct a reservoir with 275-meter high wall, in the higher reaches of the Himalaya. The observations and the consequences of these interventions have many faceted problems. They involve huge financial resource till, hydropower is generated. The social scenario chages entirely.

Above all there is an impending threat to the life of downstream people. Over the years several such major events have taken place.

Nathpa 1993 During July-August 1993, a landslide from the right bank of Sutlej obstructed the flow of Sutlej near Nathpa, 185 km from Shimla, creating an artificial lake. Water of the lake entered through the outlet of 120 MW Bhaba *Power House* causing heavy losses. During this period people in the low lying areas of the Sutlej, below that spot, spent sleepless nights.

Panvi 1997 On the evening of August 11, 1997, the Panvi Khud, a small nullah originating up in the Shatul Ghati brought tons of debris with it and blocked the mighty Sutlej for several days. Six major bridges were washed away leaving no trace and cutting the Kinnaur from rest of the country and eroding about 6 km of the NH 22. Big boulders and gravel buried the small habitation and 11 persons at Wangtu. A big lake was formed at Wangtu due to the blockage of the Sutlej. For several days people made their way to Kinnaur by crossing the artificial lake by boat.

Kailash 2000 The third incident that brought a high column of water on the August 1, 2000 occurred far away at the origin of Sutlej in Mt. Kailash, the abode of Shiva. However, the major loss took place in the region between Rampur and Wangtu. The damage would have run into several hundred crores as a direct loss to the Nathpa Jhakri Hydroelectric Project.

The environmental aspects of such changes have been utterly ignored.

In certain areas there is a severe conflict between the State policy and the policies being thrust by these agencies. For example, there is strong opposition by the outside agencies against the provision of the timber distribution rights (TD) and other forest resource used by the peasant population. Their reasoning is very simple. First, they hardly have any sense of sympathy with the problems of people of Himachal Pradesh; who are dependent on the forests not only for their material needs but also for their psychological needs. The most outrageous belief among the experts of the outside agencies is that the villagers are corrupt, forest officers accept bribe and the politicians empathize with them for the sake of votes (Bingeman, Gardner, & Sinclair, 2000). If these attitudes are going to decide the policy formulation, how do we think of eliciting people's participation? We must not forget that it was the most learned colonial ruling class that alienated people of India from their forests. Not only that, the science of silviculture is yet to develop the ethos of conservation. Some possible solutions to these issues form the content of chapters in the remaining parts of this essay. This will include some theoretical viewpoints on relationship between nature and society that has relevance to India and Himachal Pradesh in particular (Chapter 4). Next we will present our theoretical viewpoint that has emphasis on cooperative relationships in nature (Chapter 5) and the society (Chapter 6). The last chapter suggests the development of the indigenous institutions for the holistic development in the Himachal Himalaya.

4

Diversity of Views

The theory of evolution and the science of ecology, both help us to understand the behviour from a holistic viewpoint. There is no conflict between parts and whole. In fact it is difficult to define these terms without reference to each other. What is important for us is to keep in mind that to study a phenomenon we have to proceed from the top. We should not loose track of the parts that make a whole at one level but these wholes are parts of another whole at a higher level and so on. The famous evolutionary biologist, Goodwin (1996) in his book, "*How the leopard changed its spots*" describes the emergent property principle in biology. He explains the evolution of cooperation as a higher process rather in terms of the selfish gene model.

A gene has to pass through various levels of organizations in the individual itself in order to express itself, because it is behaviour (or phenotype) on which nature acts. Sometimes, it may have to go beyond the level of the individual, because the selection may take place at the level of group. There is a need to explore behaviour from various perspectives and seek help from those who are experts in seeing inside the cell and also from those who are good in observing the populations in their natural landscapes. Furthermore, it is to be communicated to a larger population. For this the socio-cognitive revolution seems a pragmatic way.

Common Wisdom

Human populations adapt to specific environmental conditions by means of socio-cultural institutions. The adaptive changes may occur at various levels: inter-individual interactions, group formation, social institutions, cultural components, socio-cultural formation, and cultural adjustment. The idea of Nature-Man-Spirit complex given by an anthropologist, Vidyarthi (1963), arose from his observations of the dependence of people in India on nature and their belief in the supernatural and the spirit world.

Other workers later had similar observations about man-nature relationship. In the upper reaches of the Himalayas, a linguist, Norberg-Hodge (1994), who has worked laboureously to save the ecology of Ladakh, described the sentiments of a villager in this way: "*Please give enough that we may worship the Buddhas and bodhisattvas; That we may support the Sangha and give to the poor*!" These thoughts are not only common among the Buddhists of Lahaul & Spiti and Kinnaur in Himachal Pradesh, but they signify a deep-rooted ethics that was part of India's culture (Bajaj & Srinivas, 1996). The ethics had been to grow more grains and to share these grains among all.

In the mid-Himalayan region the *ban*, the land not actively shaped by man, namely forests and high pastures, is divine and pure state of nature for the Banganis of northwestern Garhwal (Zoller, 1990). People of Bangan have special relations with their *ban* where they encounter their gods and fairies. The dominant deity in this region, the Tons valley, is the Mahasu. The river Tons has its tributaries in the adjacent region of Himachal Padesh. Thus it is not surprising that the Mahasu deity still has its territory up to Shimla. Despite the political divisions (the area is divided into Uttaranchal and Himachal) the people in this region have close cultural affinity due to the institution of Mahasu *devata*.

In the Shivalik hills the local (indigenous) knowledge and conventional (modern) science were complementary to each other in the context of checking soil erosion. The live example is Sukho Majri (Sarin, 1996; Scott & Walter, 1993). The local dialect contains a detailed lexicon of the habitat used by the people. There are examples of cooperative management of natural resources—such as wastelands, forests, groundwater, surface water and fisheries—that have been documented in recent past (Singh & Ballabh, 1996). People have traditional social institutions for the management of local common property resources (CPRs) that include local forest, water source, irrigation water, grazing land and various other resources which people use collectively (Prakash, 1998).

The community work of a retired school principle in the hills near Dehra Dun, that has relevance for Uttaranchal as well as

Himachal, has re-defined sustainability as the capacity of those most in need of change to take actual charge of it (Alter, 2002). In this the ecological context acquires meaning for people only through the traditional ways of life. Tradition includes opinion, belief, custom or knowledge and doctrines of divine authority handed down by ancestors to posterity (Arunachalam, 2001). There is need for an integrative approach to understand the man and nature relations. In this integrative approach we have not to loose track of the holistic view while resolving the environmental issues (Box 4.1).

We can understand the interrelationship of ecology, culture and behaviour in India following various theoretical approaches. This chapter describes several contemporary approaches to give an idea about how ecology interacts with culture to determine patterns of behaviour.

Box 4.1: Learning the science of Mother Earth

Today the cost of forest is calculated in terms of carbon.

In Himachal Pradesh carbon sink is the third major contributor to the Total Economic Value (US$22.69 billion).

Why? Because from the Gaia we learn that:

Free oxygen is largely the consequence of photosynthesis in plants. The burial of plants and animals in the soil increases the store of carbon. The drive for industrial development is putting back carbon into the atmosphere at an alarming rate. Excess carbon in atmosphere is dangerous to our survival—global warming is one such consequence.

The problem is that modern technologies have transformed the world so much that we no longer see the consequences of what we are doing.

There are few in younger generation who have curiosity about the traditional wisdom.

Evolutionary Approach

Scientists are familiar with the experimental designs developed by R.A. Fisher, but very few may be aware of the fact that his major contribution has been in developing a synthetic theory of evolution by combining the Darwinian natural selection with the Mendelian genetics. Fisher, Wright and Haldane (he later shifted to India from England) revolutionized the evolutionary theory with population genetic models. Sociobiologists and ecologists use these models to study the gene flow among populations. In India, Madhav Gadgil stimulated a number of students in the study of ecology and sociobiology at the Center for Ecological Sciences, I.I.Sc., Bangalore. Gadgil's approach to development of behaviour is strongly rooted in evolutionary biology.

A major thesis propounded by Gadgil is that a large number of communities are maintained in isolation by a complex *specialization of occupation* (Gadgil & Malhotra, 1983). A corollary of the thesis is that this specialization of function has also insulated Indians from the onslaught of invading streams of people. The Indian society has assimilated in itself the ideas and innovations. Gadgil (1991) has stated in his thesis that, "*Each subgroup of the Indian society is relatively homogeneous with all members traditionally pursuing a well defined similar mode of subsistence and having very similar level of access to resources.*" An interdisciplinary team consisting of Gadgil and his associates have analysed some of the data documented by the 'People of India' (POI) Project of the Anthropological Survey of India about each and every community of India (Singh, 2002). A total of 2,753 communities were reported in 32 state/union territories (State/UT) in India.

They adapted ecological measures to understand the diversity of communities and traits among the population of India. The *α-diversity* gave the number of traits per community (Joshi, Gadgil & Patil, 1993). The differences between communities were measured as *β-diversity,* which was the proportion of unshared traits amongst two communities. The third measure was the number of traits in a state, *the γ-diversity*, which was a function of trait richness and dissimilarity. They also looked for clusters of traits in terms of geography, social and economic factors. It was found that part of cultural diversity of the Indian subcontinent could be explained by the ecological setting which provides resources to people. There is need to use these methods for the exploration of biological and cultural diversity in Himachal Pradesh.

The above analysis revealed that the number of traits in a community ranged from 32 to 406 with a mean of 204 in 32 State/UT. Most of the communities reporting large number of traits were groups dependent directly on the natural resources. It is to be noted that the Khas (it should be Khashia) community from Himachal Pradesh has reported the highest number of traits (406).

It is also significant that the number of communities in Himachal Pradesh (116) is higher than its adjacent states—Haryana (82), Punjab

(95) and Jammu & Kashmir (111). This plurality of communities and the traits within the communities are important indicators of the rich cultural diversity in the State. Does this contribute to peace in this Himalayan state? The prevalence of peace is an important social event in recent times when we find that there is turmoil in Jammu & Kashmir, Punjab, and Uttaranchal. Himachal Pradesh has also recorded a unique achievement on the social front also—it is the socially most progressive state in India (Saran, 2004).

Some other important observations about Himachal Pradesh from POI project data analysis are as follows. The trait dissimilarity and total number of traits in the State are moderate for Himachal Pradesh. The geographical distance does not predict trait dissimilarity—Himachal Pradesh shares 50 per cent traits with Jammu & Kashmir but it also shares 56 per cent traits with the distant Assam. There is, however, some indication that the rural dominance and the traditional culture are the principal modes of life.

The correlation analysis revealed a pattern of diversity in terms of socio-economic stratification that characterize the hilly areas of western Himalayas including Himachal Pradesh. This complex of barley/maize/mustard is linked with terrace cultivation, smoking of loose tobacco, acceptance of lavirate form of marriage, participation in caste council in resolution of disputes over land, practices of exorcism and divination and attribution of putative kinship to members of other communities.

Although large number of communities still prefer traditional mode (settled agriculture), occupational diversity suggests that the traits are changing. Among the current occupations the choice is very narrow—the preference is for the government service. There is important lesson for Himachal Pradesh here. For future people need to diversify their occupational choices and work in that direction. As Amartya Sen has reiterated; the widening of the individual capabilities is important to meet the adverse environmental challenges. These challenges may be natural calamities, displacement due to large dams or to meet the needs of globalisation.

Coming back to the environmental scenario in India, Gadgil and his coworkers have combined the biological and cultural approaches in a meaningful way. Two examples that have relevance for Himachal Pradesh should suffice. The scenario of material flows that characterize Himachal Pradesh is more or less similar to the *Settled Cultivation* mode of production and resource use (Gadgil & Guha,

1993; Figure 4.1). However, a perceptible shift towards the *Industrial Mode* is taking place in the three areas: hydropower, apple cultivation and mining.

In India, there is gross inefficiency in the management of natural resources—the faulty incentive system has perpetuated in an Iron Triangle (Gadgil & Rao, 1998). There are large state-sponsored subsidies that benefit the small section of Indian democracy whereas the masses bear the costs (Figure 4.2). Perhaps due to better political and administrative structure (as compared to other states of India) in Himachal Pradesh the masses are able to get their share of benefits and have to bear lesser costs.

Fig. 4.1: The settled cultivation mode of production and resources use

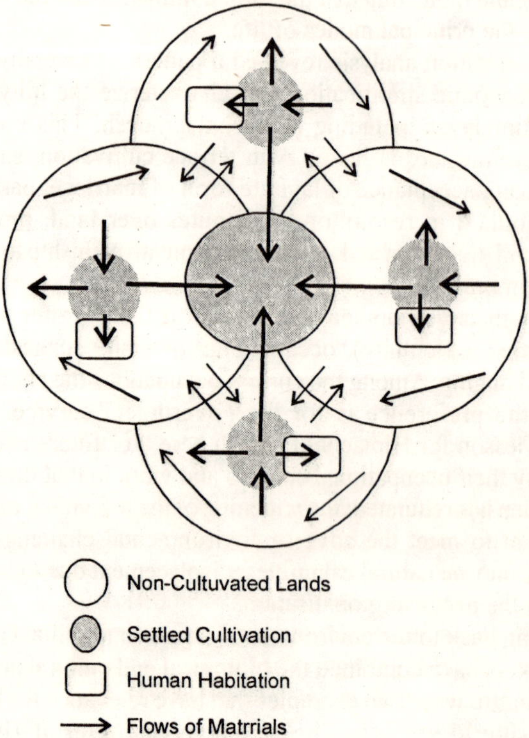

Source: Gadgil & Guha, 1993.

Fig. 4.2: The Iron Triangle, the incentive system for natural resouces use

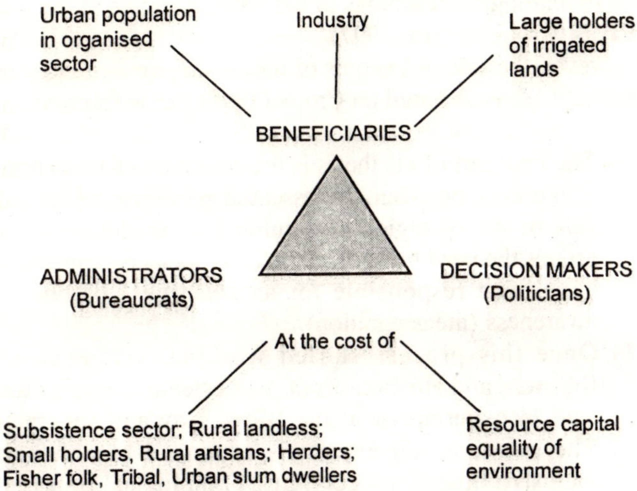

Source: Gadgil & Rao, 1998.

Socio-ecological Approach

Over the years, a socio-ecological approach (Crook, 1989) has emerged which provides a new perspective to explore how biological evolution and cultural evolution interact with each other to produce differential patterns of behaviour and adaptations in human populations and allied species. Some distinguishing features of socio-ecology are as follows.

First, the role of behaviour within a social system which itself is an ecological adaptation. Second, the way a trait spreads in a population, which involves the population genetics of the selective process. Third, the incorporation of both innate (biological) and learned (cultural) behaviours in the approach, some evolutionary psychologists believe only in the selection of innate behaviours. Fourth, the religious ideas and religious codes may sometimes determine biologically significant traits. Lastly, the important role played by psychological mechanisms that bring about biological and cultural adaptation.

The socio-ecological approach of Crook is unique in hypothesizing the psychological processes in cultural and genetic coevolution. This approach has been applied in understanding the social organization of people of Ladakh (Crook & Osmaston, 1994) and the psychological teachings of the Tibetan yogins of the western Himalayas (Crook & Low, 1997).

However, the salient features of the *social psychological model of cultural preference* based on Crook (1995) are as follows:

(*a*) The first part of his thesis is the evolution of mind and self. This according to him was essential to understand the cultural side of the biological and cultural co-evolution. In social groups the need for self-reference in social encounters might have been responsible for an awareness of one's own awareness (metacognition).

(*b*) Once this process started working, self-evaluations followed and attributions of high esteem to one's own self lead to experiences of the 'flow' (joy and satisfaction). The positive self-esteem is supposed to enhance the inclusive fitness, a special case of biological fitness of the individual (Figure 4.3).

(*c*) However, it is determined by the ecological conditions and societal norms and values; the more they are tied to the subsistence base, the more likely is to be the fit between the individual and his biological adaptation and greater would be the experience of the flow (higher inclusive fitness).

(*d*) On the other hand social disapproval and poor match of the societal norms with the ecological conditions would lead to poor well-being (lower inclusive fitness).

(*e*) The situation becomes complex; where the social cultural changes are initiated group selection processes start acting. A minority group may perceive itself to be deprived; such processes may lead to social breakdown and conflicts. Individuals may experience low self-esteem and loss of identity.

(*f*) Crook has emphasized the socio-economic contexts of belief and the role of religious institutions in it (Figure 4.4). This is important for the concept of 'niche construction', which is a cultural adaptation. The concept of niche is widely used in ecology, but Crook defines 'niche size' as the extent to which a religion captures the personal world of individuals. Other contextual variables are also important.

Fig. 4.3: Relations between societal values, ideology, adaptation and fitness

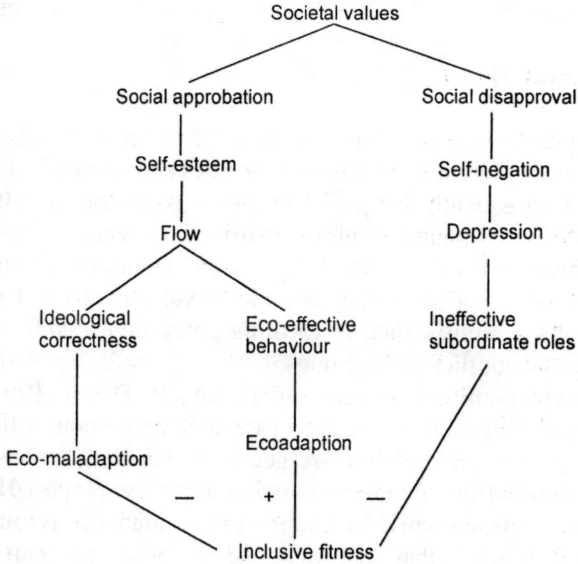

Source: Crook, 1995.

Fig. 4.4: Relations between societal values, self-identification and esteem

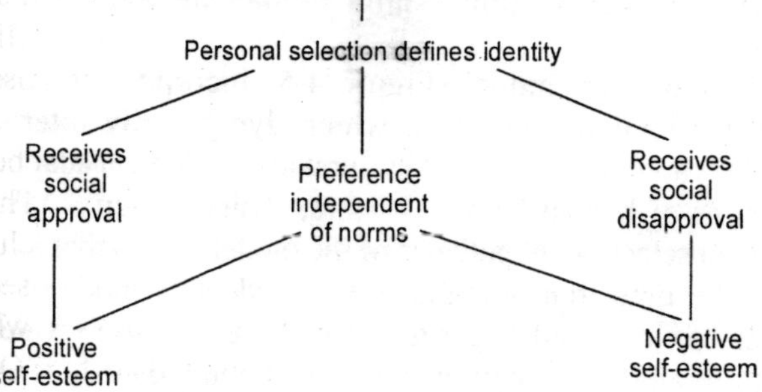

Source: Crook, 1995.

(*g*) The model has been tested in analysing the cultural adaptations of the Buddhists living in the Himalaya including Ladakh.

Eco-cultural Model

In their pursuit to search universal laws of behavior, psychologists have been indifferent to flourishing societies and cultures in diverse terrains. Consequently, the public image of psychology as a helping profession has remained a mirage (Misra & Gergen, 2001; Segall, Dasen, Berry & Poortinga, 1999). The social, cultural and contextual variables are important as they provide 'developmental niche' for a child or have significance in creating antecedent conditions for harmony and conflict in the groups.

The cross-cultural psychologists, Segall, Dasen, Berry and Poortinga (1999) have explored them as parallel evolutionary tracks—the biological and the cultural—respectively signifying the biological transmission and the cultural transmission. They have proposed a broad eco-cultural framework to understand human behaviour. The framework suggests that ecological and socio-cultural contexts are important and influence various aspects of human psychology. But they are also very clear that all earlier arguments of the greater superiority of human beings from their biological relatives have been challenged.

These cross-cultural psychologists however report strong evidence that human beings continue to carry their evolutionary adaptation, but it does not undermine the thesis that human behaviour is shaped in socio-cultural context. In this process learning plays the central role. The eco-cultural framework of Segall et al provides a cross-cultural approach to understand human behaviour in global perspective.

The theoretical model (Figure 4.5) incorporates contextual variables, social and cultural, which dynamically interact with ecological variables and lead to cultural and biological adaptations in populations of human beings (Mishra, Sinha & Berry, 1996). The 'adaptation selection' hypothesis of the model argues that as cultures evolve over time from a nomadic to a sedentary mode of life, the demands of closer and larger group living emphasise greater social conformity and sensitivity at the cost of individual independence (Mishra & Tripathi, 1996; Shreshtha & Mishra, 1996). The sedentary society permits greater role diversity in the community at large and greater role specialization among individuals.

Fig. 4.5: The eco-cultural model

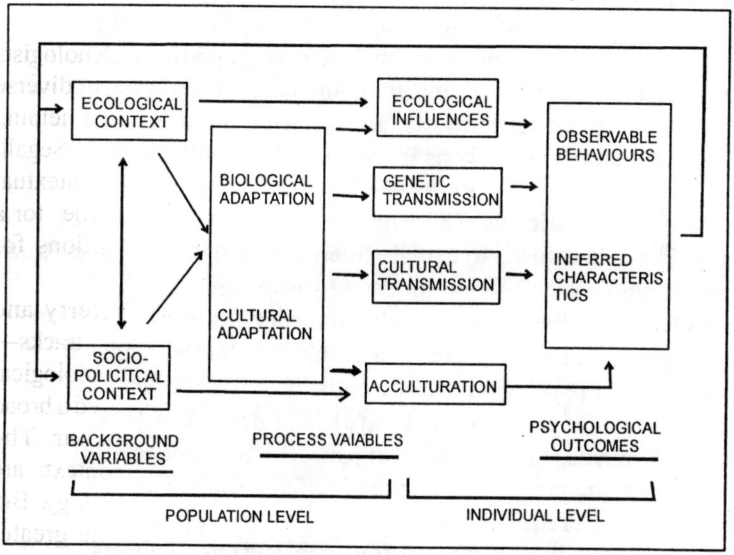

Source: Mishra, Sinha & Berry, 1996.

A lot of evidence has gathered following the eco-cultural model, which strongly supports certain relationships between ecology and behaviour (Mishra, 2000; Segall et al., 1999). Two examples are here: the link of eco-cultural context to cognitive style and cognitive development is very clear; and, socialization practices mediate the influence of group-level variables on individual functioning. Experience with groups belonging to other cultures leads to acculturation. In general, the eco-cultural variables affect the way we perceive the world. However, the cultural adaptation of the eco-cultural model (Berry et al., 1987; Segall et al., 1999) is needed and some attempts have already been made in India (Mishra, Sinha & Berry, 1996).

The eco-culture model is popular among cross-cultural psychologists and has been employed in large variety of studies. A major drawback of this approach is its poor linkage with contemporary models of evolution of behavior and environmental issues. For our purpose here, the following argument derived from the eco-cultural model is important. The groups or communities differ according to eco-cultural characteristics and levels of acculturation. In our cognition, the transfer of information from one sensory modality to the other is common. However it is possible that the routine use of visual sense modality in the forest increases higher level of differentiation for structural properties—shape, size and height. Thus the possibility of spatial analysis is very high in the nomadic hunter-gatherer groups. But there may be heavy demand for surface analysis in the settled agriculturist families. A variety of household material need surface analysis—cloth, wood, glass, metal, plastic, etc. These hypotheses based on the eco-cultural model have been used to explain intermodel differences in cultural groups who have different modes of subsistence.

On similar lines, the eco-cultural model has been used to study some groups or communities in Himachal Pradesh. Broadly this analysis—the psychological differentiation—has been made in terms of two types of cognitive styles: (*a*) field dependent (FD)—where whole dominates the perception of parts, (*b*) field independent (FI)—where parts are perceived irrespective of the whole. Sagar Sharma at the Himachal Pradesh University has used this approach to analyse the cognitive abilities in students from rural and urban habitats (Sharma & Ahuja, 1981; 1990) and between Tibetan and Indian communities (Sharma & Dogra, 1988).

In his address to the social scientists of India, psychologist Sharma cautioned that the displacement is likely to erode the traditional psychological support systems and consequently reduce the capacity of individuals, families and communities to cope up with distress, disease and diversity (Sharma, 1994). Considering his vast experience in the area of stress and anxiety, these factors remain to be explored among the huge number of displaced people in Himachal Pradesh. Furthermore, the deleterious consequences of stress and anxiety in populations from various habitats and cultural backgrounds are an area of wide practical significance. For example, how do the transhumant people of Kinnaur face the challenge of acculturation? Or, would a student from Kinnaur have more test-anxiety than a student from Shimla? If a student from Kinnaur is likely to have more test-anxiety, what measures are required to cope up with it?

Human Ecology Approach

In this approach the emphasis is to understand the social systems as parallel to the eco-systems. Most of the approaches in ecology have neglected the role of social systems. The emphasis on the social systems is best illustrated in Marten's (2001) *Human ecology: Basic concepts for sustainable development.* The main points of this approach are outlined here and it has relevance for Himachal Pradesh since the issues taken up in this volume by Marten approximate the problems of developing countries, including India.

A. Human ecology studies the relationship between people and their environment. The human beings constitute the social system whereas the environment is perceived as the ecosystem (Figure 4.6). The central concept in human ecology is the social system having demographic, social and psychological properties. Marten has discussed in detail the cooking fuel and deforestation in India to illustrate the interaction of the social system and eco-system.

Fig. 4.6: Interaction between eco-system and social system

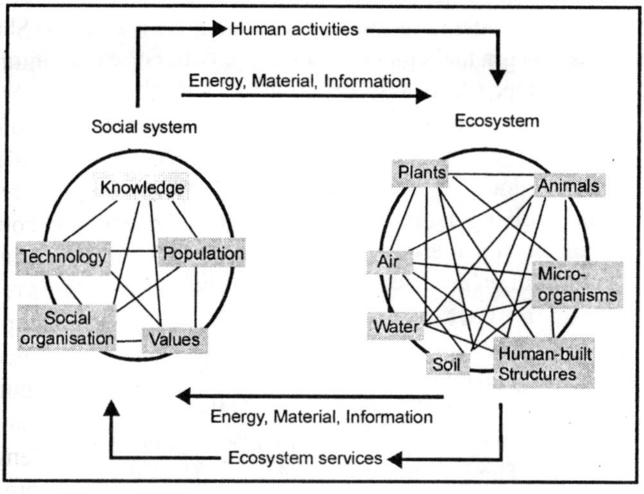

Source: Marten, 2001.

B. The ecosystem and social system function and interact as

self-organizing, complex adaptive systems. They promote survival in a dynamic environment. The concept of emergent property is introduced to understand human-environment interactions at various levels. These emergent properties may be biological, social and psychological and originate at individual as well as group level. Some examples of emergent properties are: self-organisation, stability or homeostasis, complexity, coadaptation (fitting together), coevolution (changing together), cooperation or symbiosis and denial.

C. Although population growth beyond carrying capacity is a major problem, the enormous consumption by wealthy nations also exhausts the resources. Attempts are needed to discover social mechanisms of population regulation. Three points are important here: look for the traditional wisdom to control population; territoriality as an evolutionary mechanism for the regulation of number of individuals; and, the humanistic ways of pushing the limits of carrying capacity of the earth. The last one needs cognitive revolution directed towards control of population through culturally sensitive ways, reduction in consumption rates, egalitarian use of resources and defining the parameters of the quality of life.

D. From co-adaptaion between social system and ecosystem, there is gradual co-evolution of the two. For example, at the subsistence level farmers co-adapt with the natural system and there is very little modification of the latter one. However, after the technological revolution the human impact has been tremendous. In fact, now the social system and eco-system are evolving under the human control. It is here that various fallacies have arisen. Two such opposing tendencies about our future have been discussed in Chapter 2—the selfish model of development and the altruistic model of development.

E. People make sense of complexity of their surroundings in terms of physical, social and self related perceptions. These perceptions are observed in the form of stories and images in minds. The information about eco-system is perceived, it is interpreted and modified to make decision in a social system. The five common perceptions of nature are: (*a*) Everything is connected; (*b*) Benign/perverse (nature is kind/nature is cruel); (*c*) Fragile (nature has delicate balance); (*d*) Durable (largely nature is stable); and, (*e*) Capricious (nature is unpredictable).

F. Sustainable human-eco-system interaction involves two things. We have to follow nature's way and not to damage eco-systems. The social systems have two important properties—resilience and adaptive development. Resilience is the ability of social systems and eco-systems to continue functioning despite severe and unexpected changes. This ability is enhanced by adaptive development processes, which are aimed at coping up with change.

This is possible by development of social institutions for sustainable use of common property resources. One possibility is to look at the traditional religious institutions to play important role. For Marten (2001) "*Religion is a way in which societies use generations of accumulated wisdom to organize their values, perceptions and behaviour.*" Group ownership is part of it, however new ways of conflict resolution are to be evolved. There must be emphasis on the cooperative use of resources.

Multidisciplinary Approach

A. Theoretical Issues

This is characterized by the introduction to plurality of methods of analysis and of issues related to sustainable development. However the integration remains elusive. The main focus is to explore the link between sustainability and the problem of overpopulation. The first part in this section describes Anup Shah's (1998) approach to explain the population growth of human species with relation to natural environment. He integrates the insights of analytical economics and behavioural ecology. The main concern is the decrease in resiliency of the natural environment as a consequence of population growth.

He starts with the biological concept of niche. Niches in the natural world are assumed like the professions in an economy, e.g., the cheetah's niche in the forest and the teacher's profession in the universities. A given niche can support only a limited number of niche spaces. A niche space is like a territory for a breeding pair or the pride of lions. In nature there is perfect control on the number of niche spaces or the number of individuals in an area. However the institutional innovations in human beings have created narrow niche-spaces in addition to the broad niche-spaces.

It is assumed that there is relationship between the niche-spaces and the population size. People who are able to acquire broad niche-spaces have access to more resources. But the number of broad niche-spaces is fewer than the narrow niche-spaces. As a result of which most of the people are confined to narrow niche-spaces having scarcity of resources. This is explained by the ancient caste system in India. The higher castes enjoyed the broad niche-spaces whereas the lower castes survived in the narrow niche spaces. Furthermore, in the lower sections of society the mechanism evolved for population control can probably be called infanticide.

Shah proposes that the technology revolution has played important role in broadening the niche-spaces. However, the growing human population soon fills these niche-spaces. Thus effort is wasted. The main theme of the monograph by Shah is the technological progress and its potential to raise human welfare. This western optimism in technology overlooks the role of the human desire to use more and more resources. Whereas the cognitive revolution advocated in the present report places emphasis on two things, the increase in the quality of life through human wisdom and the control of human desire by observing austerity in the use of resources.

The principle of peaceful coexistence is important for the biological communities but the human beings have broken it through cultural evolution. It has taken a turn where each individual attempts to amass niches and in doing so denies food and space to others. This drive on one hand led to prosperity in the Western world but the societies following the principle of coexistence remained poor, surviving in impoverished niches. The most important achievement by the Western world was the *demographic transition*—from high mortality and high fertility rates to low mortality and low fertility rates. A major thesis advocated on the basis of this demographic transition is that prosperity changes fertility behaviour.

The preceding phenomenon observed in the West is used by Shah to develop economic models of fertility behavior that may possibly help a similar transition in the developing countries. The reasoning is based on the behaviour of rational, selfish couples that respond to changes in the environment in which they live. The hypothetical cases of the *Chicago couple* and the *Rajasthan couple* are compared. It is concluded that the net costs of children are lower and benefits higher in the third world than in the West. In other words the direction of transfer of resources (benefits from children) decides whether a country has made demographic transition or not (Figure 4.7).

Fig. 4.7: Decision making by couples

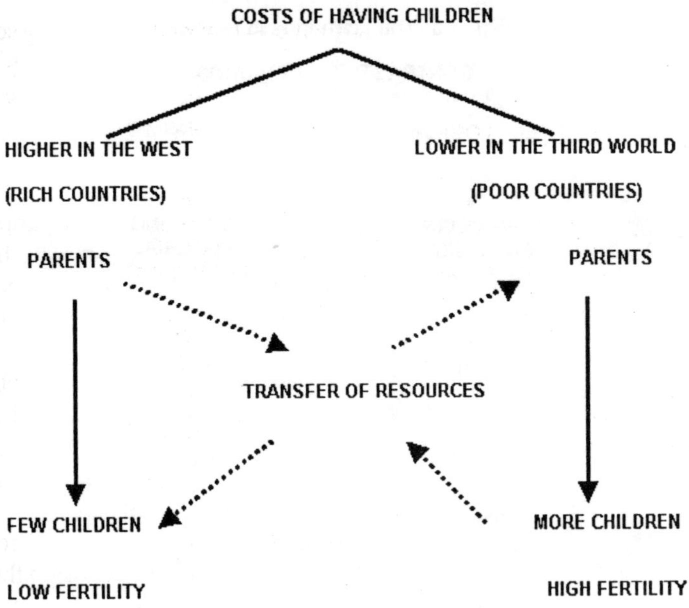

Source: Shah, 1998.

There is strong evidence that overcrowding negatively affects the quality of life in terms of its three ingredients: space, liberty and the absence of stress, tension and anxiety. Shah also considers the issue of self-regulation of family size at individual and community level. He borrows the socio-biological (Chapter 5) model of Trivers based on genetic relatedness, reciprocation and decision-making. Using rational decision-making and the repeated prisoner's dilemma game Shah concludes that the self-regulation of family size may be possible. However considering the scenario in the natural world he discards it because over the years there has been erosion of the social norms that encourage cooperation. His final argument is summarized in the Figure 4.8 in favour of the selfish economic model.

The present report however provides more evidence on the cooperative behaviour from natural populations of primates (Chapter 5) and it is followed by two examples from the more dynamic scenario from human social institutions where cooperation among people leads to decision making relevant to solve various issues related to environment (Chapters 6 and 7).

Fig. 4.8: The scenarios in real world

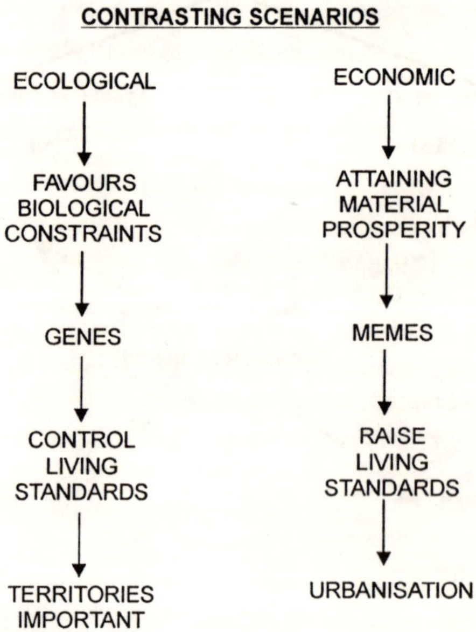

Source: Shah, 1998.

B. Practical Issues

The second part of this section describes the viewpoint of another alarmist, Ragini Sen (2003). For her the population growth is a time bomb but she does not know the exact time limit of its explosion. Her conclusions about the causes and possible remedies of the problem are non-complementary with those of Anup Shah described above.

But this is an important addition to the multidisciplinary approach described above specifically on the issue of the population stabilization. She has followed the European model of social psychology as opposed to the American model of social psychology. Particularly the theory of collective representation propounded by Durkhiem and later by Moscovici is used to analyse the social representations of people about family planning in India. In her elaborate qualitative analysis of the role of social and cultural factors in the population stabilization in India there are important lessons on three issues.

(*a*) The approach should be holistic, she opposes the game theory models such as used by Shah and others.

(*b*) There should be emphasis on soft cultural factors (which are generally ignored, e.g., the slogans used in family planning campaigns); for this an understanding of local cultural factors is essential.

(*c*) Literacy of women is particularly important in reducing the atrocity on women; it is ultimately the empowerment of women that would increase the sex-ratio and reduce the fertility ratio.

(*d*) The myth that over-population is a creation of "minorities" needs to be demystified. It is a significant issue but needs more evidence from primary sources.

(*e*) Her strategy for population stabilization includes grassroots level research on success stories in the problem states such as Bihar, Uttar Pradesh, Rajasthan, etc. Thus the emphasis is to develop indigenous models of population stability that may even vary within the state.

There are, however, two important lessons for Himachal Pradesh in the study of Ragini Sen. The first lesson is related to the census data of 2001 where unexpectedly Himachal Pradesh has also joined some other states where the child sex-ratio was low. There is sharp decline in the 0 to 6 years sex-ratio in Punjab, Haryana, Himachal Pradesh, Gujrat, Chandigarh and Delhi. She blames dowry for this decline in the child sex-ratio.

Her second argument is that the fertility rates in both Kerala and Goa are lower than those recorded in the USA—1.99 in the corresponding year. This empirical evidence is an indicator, where Himachal Pradesh may also join, that fertility rates are more dependent on social welfare and empowerment of women. Furthermore, neither do citizens of developing countries nor do minorities create the tragedy of commons.

Lastly, Ragini Sen has emphasized the unity of mind and body with relation to fertility issues. She has shown that social representations of fertility, body (corporeity) and health-illness are interlinked. She has strongly advocated that on the basis of these findings—that social representations play a central role in fertility behaviour and they are not only affected by objective and scientific information but also by cultural factors—it is clear that policies related to reproductive health and population stabilization must consider the socio-psychological factors.

An important point that runs throughout her book (Sen, 2003) is her concern for the common person's viewpoints (*philosophia plebia*) in understanding the problem and in finding out the solutions. These in association with the collective beliefs are key to the formation of any policy that needs to involve the billion people inhabiting Indian landscape. In the present essay the last two chapters address this issue in detail with reference to some environmental issues in the northwest Himalaya.

The following chapters are intended to provide more evidence on:

(*a*) Biological basis of cooperation from non-human primate groups;
(*b*) Native wisdom where cooperative strategy is used to resolve environmental conflicts; and,
(*c*) Role of the institution of deity in community development.

5

Evolution of Cooperation

The nature of interactions is very important and is related to the way of life of the people. The way of life in any particular place differs from the other places in the region, in the country or on the planet Earth. There are some strands that are common but largely people innovate their own ways. It is with regard to these innovations based upon people's learning and experience on one hand and on the basis of history, culture and other aspects of social life on the other hand.

It is obvious that the interactions that are taking place between the two individuals, two groups or two nations differ according to numerous factors associated with the interacting parties. Our objective, however, is to formulate the essential nature of the interactions and the desired outcome. For example, the humanist orientation of this essay conceptualizes cooperative interactions rather than the competitive interactions for sustainable development. The objective is the same for humanist as well as other approaches. In the area of environment, for example, it may be the conservation of forests and wildlife. We present in the next chapter the success story of the Chipko Movement (hug- the-tree movement) that has its origin in the Northwest Himalayas. Some social workers from Himachal Pradesh were also actively involved in this movement.

Need for Cooperative Social System

This brings in several important questions that are considered significant in all the societies. These are related to human perceptions about their preferences to adopt a way of life; given that there are various ways of life. The choice of preferences may go down to finer levels. Consider for example a person's interaction with his infant. Is the love of a mother to her child different in a monkey, in a person living in an isolated Himalayan village and a person who has a lot of material resources? Following the humanistic way of life we assume that the nature of love is similar in these three mother-infant interactions—the monkey, the materially poor and the materially rich.

There is however a dominant view which while considering the various interventions to stabilize the population growth seem to condemn the love of monkey mother and the materially poor mother in comparison to the love of a materially rich mother. This dominant view holds the opinion that these differences will vanish when the society achieves egalitarianism on the basis of material approach and most of the problems, including the physical, social and psychological would be automatically resolved, once a particular level of prosperity is achieved by a country. Currently the standard of this material prosperity is considered equivalent to the one that is prevalent in the European countries and the United States or the developed world in general, where the rate of population growth is almost zero.

The historical evidence however indicates that the demographic transition (from high mortality and high fertility to low mortality and low fertility) that has occurred in the developed world may have partly used large amounts of natural resources extracted from all over the world. This significant achievement by the developed world is also related to the growth of science and technology and its efficient dissemination and use.

The contrasting scenario assumed by the humanists is *not* that they are averse to the development of science and technology but they consider it important to have moral and ethical constraint on it. For example, on one hand we are spending huge amounts of money to curtail fertility but on the other hand there is significant expenditure to increase the libido and impart a baby to those who are biologically not fit to have it. More important, for the humanistic approach, is to develop mechanisms of individual and collective constraints on the use of natural resources. Humanists believe that it is possible to have greater mental satisfaction and pleasure even with lesser amount of material things. But it does mean that material things are not necessary.

If the hedonistic theory is even partially true (that the human beings aspire for pleasure and they want to avoid pain), the pathway suggested by humanist approach may be more appropriate for the sustainable development rather than the pathway of high prosperity. Besides the urge for pleasure and the need to avoid pain there are some higher motives, too. They include the pathway of spiritual journey. There is yet another objective that is common to humanist approach as well as to the followers of materialist viewpoint. Both consider it important that all have to unite together and solve various environmental and the other developmental issues by following a cooperative approach. Consequently, the cooperative interactions that are taking place anywhere may vary from those within the nuclear family to the endeavours of some global forum (Box 5.1).

Box 5.1: New and the old learn from each other

The empty castle of the Rana of Darkoti, a village in Shimla hills, became alive when the peasants gathered on the return of the Goddess Durga from pilgrimage to Haridwar. Large number of people along with three deities came to greet the Durga.

On another occasion, the village has been host to the Global Ecology students from the America. For the alien community the Christmas celebrations with the villagers was warm. The American students joined hands with the men and women in the *mala* dance.

Consider the family in a Himalayan village that collects firewood daily from its vicinity. This behaviour may be perceived dangerous for the environment than the use of natural gas as a fuel for cooking food. Both these fuels are dependent on the organic matter, which is limited. The former mode of using fuel is considered traditional whereas the latter mode of fuel is considered advanced. However, classifying the fuel into traditional and advanced modes does not resolve the main issue. The solution to resolve the main issue involves a number of things—efficient use of fuel, selection of food items that consume less fuel, cultural preferences for food items to be cooked (curtailing certain preferences), quantity of consumption on various occasions, and several other things.

In some areas of Shimla in Himachal Pradesh, people in villages have often noticed that it was more time consuming to cook soyabean as more fuel was required to cook it and people do not relish its taste. But there was enormous propaganda to introduce soyabean. Such activities led to perceptions among people that some exotic varieties were being introduced in their areas by the prosperous countries with some vested interests.

Looking from the viewpoint of environment, even the use of natural gas is not a good option. First, it is a fossil fuel and is limited in supply. Secondly, there is very high subsidy that the government is providing on the natural gas cylinders provided to the users through private gas agencies or through the public distribution system. If the family, which picks up the dead/dry wood from the forest is considered as a free rider the family in the urban area purchasing a gas cylinder is a greater free rider (considering the subsidized rates of the gas cylinder).

Not only that, the children in the family of a peasant are considered as the hands furthering the deterioration of environment since they also help the family in the collection of the dead/dry wood. However we rarely consider the fact that they hardly have huge stores of the collected wood as we find in the urban centers. Largely the fuel wood by the peasant family is collected for daily use, except in higher mountains where it may be stored to meet the needs of the winter season when there is snowfall. On the other hand, the hoarding behaviour in the urban areas is not only gigantic but at times it has been misused to starve the needy population.

Although the preceding example may not be of great interest to many, it is significant to the people of Himachal Pradesh. The analysis of such interactions need great care and we have to go beyond the statistical figure of the total number of trees consumed for fuel wood by the materially poor people. They involve the fundamental cooperative man-man and man-nature interactions. We need to observe the peasant family while collecting wood or lopping the branches of tree for fodder. Whether the family takes care not to harm the regeneration of trees or disturbs the ecological balance? Whether they take interest in the preservation and propagation of those trees, which are useful for firewood, fodder and other purposes? There is overwhelming evidence that these people are extremely careful in their attitude and behaviour and also in their traditions for maintaining the cooperative interaction with the living and the non-living.

Furthermore, the social and religious institutions in the Himalayas give various indications in their traditions and wisdom that might be considered pro-environment from the present view of sustainable development. Some examples of these pro-environment traditions and wisdom may be found in the current literature on the environment. The study reported in the last chapter of this study considers this issue and shows that the institution of deity in the villages is the example of transition from myth to reality. We assume this transition was a continuous process, but most of the activities in these villages have become fossilized at some point of time.

This may have happened with the temple as the institution of knowledge. However, at some stage it was relegated to the position of a place where only some religious performances were observed. The knowledge was now provided in the educational institutions where the new manpower was developed to serve the society, and at the same time the institution of deity was isolated from the society. Later this new class, the educated class, even started classifying societies as advanced or backward; educated or uneducated; scientific or traditional; etc.

All this has happened during a slow process. These educational institutions grew in the urban centers and in this way from the decentralized system of knowledge there was a transfer to the centralized system of knowledge to meet the needs of growing urban population. Thus the villages scattered in the vast rural landscape became devoid of the sources of knowledge. It is only now that education is trickling down to the village level, but that too at an elementary level. Still we find in India, a great inequality in the availability of the centers of knowledge. Certain areas are highly impoverished as far as the centers of modern knowledge are concerned. Although Himachal Pradesh has achieved remarkable success as far as elementary education is concerned, the centers of higher learning are, however, rare in the state.

If we accept the dominant world-view that material prosperity is necessary for the demographic transition, the cognitive revolution seems to be an important way to achieve it. On the other hand, the humanist approach is not averse to higher cognitive and mental growth levels. Rather, the humanists are the strong advocates of the socio-cognitive revolution, the major factor in the stabilization of population growth. In this way, for the humanists the alternative to material prosperity is the achievement of the higher levels of cognitive and mental growth.

Here the conflict between the traditional and the modern vanishes, since the humanists as well as the materialists value knowledge. There are, however, differences over the materialist way of life and the spiritualist way of life. The tradition favours the latter way. In order to avoid such a conflict, and to take benefit of the cultural heritage, probably the wiser step is to re-establish the traditional institution of deities, as centers for community's mental health. Where the mental health is not simply the lack of mental illness but it is positive deviance. In other words, it is a way for higher cognitive and mental growth.

The other qualities needed for this transition are kindness, care, prudence, happiness, fulfillment and peacefulness. It also assumes respect for other human beings as well as for the nature and curtailment of physical, social and psychological needs. These may all be considered characteristics of positive deviance, which may be an essential aspect of the sustainable society.

In the humanist approach, there is no conflict between the tradition and the science or the old and the new, or the biological and the cultural heritage. There is always a transition from myth to reality. This is a harmonious way of life which avoids conflict between the backward and the advanced, the rural and the urban or the creation of other discriminatory categories. There is an attempt at individual level as well as at the group level to achieve this harmony. Thus the whole emphasis is on the cohesive nature of the society where cooperative rather than the competitive interactions are valued.

These social mechanisms are also considered important in our interactions with the other living and non-living entities of the world. There is an implicit assumption that these man-man interactions generalize to man-nature interactions. In other words, the harmonious social system based on cooperative interactions would lead to harmonious eco-system, which is sustainable.

In the humanist approach there is also emphasis to learn from nature. For example, attempt has been made here to provide evidence on the cooperative nature of human beings from the studies on the cooperative life of monkeys. There is vast literature in various disciplines of our art and culture where the *vanar* (monkey like creatures) have occupied important role in myth and reality. We present here evidence from the social life of the two species of monkeys, the rhesus monkey (*Macaca mulatta*) and the Hanuman langur (*Presbytis entellus*), to develop an integrative approach to ecosystem where cooperative interactions are valued.

Integrative Approach

A community based holistic approach involves the study of group dynamics; cooperative interdependence is a basic characteristic of the group and is denoted by cohesiveness among the members. On the basis of our research on the mechanisms of group cohesiveness among Indian monkeys, we have arrived at the structure of interdependence for the primate group by exploring three social psychological hypotheses, originally proposed for human groups by Deutsch (1973): *substitutability*, *positive cathexis* and *positive inducibility* (Pirta, 1990; 2002). These hypotheses, respectively, predict that in a more cooperative (cohesive) group there would be more division of labour, greater friendliness, and more attentiveness to one another. Our environmental problems generally involve conflicts between individual and collective preferences. These conflicts of interest involve human groups in the vast landscape of India (Gadgil, 2001). Gadgil's evolutionary approach to resolve environmental issues in India has ecological and cultural basis (Chapter 4; Pirta, Gadgil & Kharshikar, 1997) and encompasses the grassroots movements for the preservation of environment (Gadgil & Rao, 1998).

The main observations on the cooperative life of monkeys from our field studies in various parts of India, and specifically in Himachal Pradesh, are summarized here along with its implications for the human groups.

Nowhere in the literature on primates, would one find such a simple and factual description of the basic causes, which force the individual for group life, as given in the following lines of Frieda Housewirth Das. She observed and sketched the natural life of men and monkeys in Orissa, during 1920-1929 and described it in her book "*Leap-Home and Gentlebrawn*" (1932). A young Hanuman langur monkey has lost all its group members in an environmental tragedy (famine in the region), and was left alone.

"*He shot down to a branch thirty feet below ... far beyond any possible danger from the serpent, ... for a little isolated monkey there is no spot free from danger in all the wide world of jungle .... Then he fell to work most assiduously at grooming his neglected fur... Fragments of leaves, bits of tiny twigs, ... It was impossible for Leap-Home to get out that thorn, ... only dexterous fingers and keen eyes of another Hanuman have rendered him that service ... He broke into a prolonged wailing call ... no answer reached his ears. ... But out of the sky there dropped with folded wings like a plummet another deadly enemy, Baldhead the Eagle. He ... crashed headlong down into the thick foliage of the trees ... stillness again ... stars were sparkling ... Far off spotted deer was barking. That meant, a leopard ... Leap-Home's shivering increased uncontrollably ... The night felt frightfully*

... Never before had he known how much he needed ... to be near Gentlebrawn, strong king and father, no matter how swift and harsh his quick punishments, to be near Chatterjoy with her long encircling arms!" pp. 172-182.

Our Darwinian Kinship

Charles Darwin (1859) noticed that there was "*one special difficulty, which first appeared to me insuperable and actually fatal to my whole theory.*" This difficulty was the social structure of insect communities and especially the presence of neuters or sterile females in it.

" *... these neuters often differ widely in instinct and in structure from both the males and fertile females, and yet, from being sterile, they cannot propagate their kind ... It may well be asked how is it possible to reconcile this case with the theory of natural selection? ... This difficulty, though appearing insuperable, is lessened, or as I believe, disappears, when it is remembered that selection may be applied to family, as well as to the individual, and may thus gain the desired end.*" (Darwin, 1859; pp. 256-257).

It indicates that the traits of an individual beneficial for the survival of other group members are also selected and transmitted from generation to generation. In the colony of insects, the neuters work for the survival of their whole community and fertile males and females transmit to their fertile offspring a tendency to produce these sterile members. Thus there are two major forces at work in the evolution of social life—the one is for the survival of individual and the other for the survival of the group. The first is achieved by competing with others, for which the individual is endowed with aggressive potential while the second aim is achieved by cooperating with others for which the individual is endowed with the tendencies for mutual aid.

During the course of evolution, the animal societies have achieved a balance between two conflicting forces, i.e. "cooperation" and "disoperation" or "aggression" and "cooperation" or "cooperation" and "competition" or "egoistic" and "altruistic" drives. In the post-Darwinian era more attention was paid to emphasize the role of competition in the form of aggressive-submissive relations.

Group Life

Group size, group composition and home range are the adaptive social structures (or behaviors) in primates resulting from complex selection pressures (Crook, 1970). Living in a group is advantageous for an individual in various ways. Without even actively cooperating with other individuals of the group, he is benefited in the following manner.

(*a*) Each individual has to locate its food source. By living in a group he may be benefited by observing others. Thus as the member of individuals in the group increases, the probability of locating the food resources also increases.

(*b*) Each individual has to keep watch on predator, which takes time. This time can be saved, if the number of individuals in a group increases. As a result of it greater time can be spent in foraging, resting and other social activities.

(*c*) In a group an individual can save its chances of being preyed upon by a predator by choosing several strategies, i.e., staying in between two individuals or in the centre of several individuals.

(*d*) Suppose the predator pressure is constant at a certain place. Now if there are only few individuals the surviving ratio will decrease and the population will die. If large number of individuals comes to that place, the survival rate will be high and population will consistently increase.

(*e*) An individual can have a direct and regular access to opposite sex.

(*f*) The possibility of learning new skills will increase with increase in the number of individuals in the group.

Home Range

The size of home range varies from a few hundred square meters in a temple to five square kilometers in a forest. In general the monkey groups living in low food availability and scattered resources have larger home ranges than those living in areas where food is localized and abundant. In forest areas larger groups occupy bigger home ranges. However in urban areas the large and small groups have home ranges more or less same in size. The home ranges of adjacent groups overlap considerably.

A group derives many advantages by living in a home range.

(*a*) Living in an area year after year group members can easily locate the food sources, water sources and safe places.

(*b*) Group becomes acquainted with the ways of potential predators of that particular area and can avoid them.

(*c*) In scarcity of food in, one part of home range, they can easily move to other part, without expenditure of energy and time in searching the routes.

(*d*) The selection of core areas inside home ranges also has advantages. These areas mostly contain rich food supply, roosting sites, safe places and water sources.

Living Cooperatively

Monkeys living in urban and forest areas spontaneously exhibit different types of cooperative behaviours to meet the exigencies of environment. However, all age-sex classes do not participate equally in all types of cooperative activities. The environmental exigencies can be divided into two kinds. First, those arising from external environment of the group, which comprise the intergroup, interspecies and all other ecological factors. Second, those arising from the internal environment, which comprise the social environment developed as a result of living together of individuals in a group. In other words, the first type of environment forces the individuals to work together so that they can meet its challenges more successfully and beneficially. The second type of environment, however, forces the individuals to develop and maintain this togetherness consistently, over a time period.

In the groups of the two species of monkeys we found five types of cooperative behaviours that are exhibited by group members in order to meet the exigencies of environment. These are the various ways, which monkeys in the urban and forest areas, adopt to meet the external challenges, after the genesis of cooperation. There are seven other kinds of cooperative behaviors that are exhibited by group members to meet the exigencies of internal environment. Those are the ways by which monkeys develop and maintain cooperativeness inside the group. The ethological observations on the cooperative life of monkeys (Pirta, 1983; 1984a, b) are described below. The genesis, development and maintenance of cooperation is shown diagrammatically as follows (Figure 5.1).

Fig. 5.1: Cooperative interdependence in a primate group

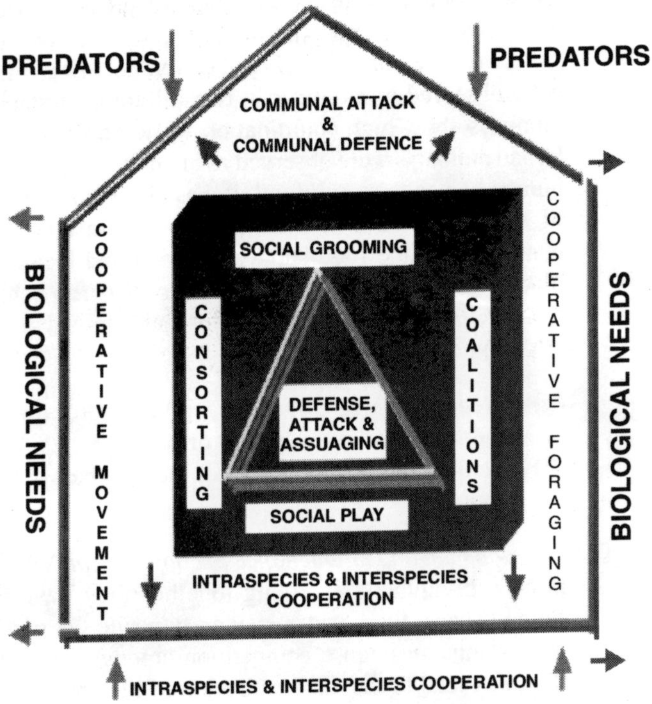

A. *Genesis of cooperation*: The monkeys live in groups and home ranges which differ in their size in different ecological conditions. The group life evolved millions of years ago and it offers several advantages for an individual. The need to meet the challenges of external environment is probably the basic cause that may have forced the members of a group in the genesis of various ways of cooperation.

The five types of cooperative behaviours observed in urban and forest monkeys to cope with the external environment are: interspecies and intraspecies cooperation, cooperative foraging, cooperative movement, communal attack and communal defence. The monkeys, both in urban and forest areas, live with other animals. Forest monkey groups have developed cooperative relationships with langurs and other rhesus groups living in the same area. Both species (rhesus and langur) and two groups of same species (rhesus-rhesus) communicate the approach of predators with each other by giving alarm calls.

Two different types of cooperative foraging behaviours were observed in monkeys in two different habitats. Forest monkeys show high coordination while raiding crop fields. Urban monkeys were observed as attacking cooperatively on human beings to snatch food. It was observed that members of a group in both habitats tolerated themselves in close contact when the food supply was rich and located in one place. All this indicates the evolution of two new behavioural characteristics in urban monkeys for their survival in the urban environment.

(*a*) Potential for aggressive behaviour towards members of other group of same species or other species.
(*b*) Potential for tolerance towards the members of their own group.

B. *Development and maintenance of cooperation*: When two or more individuals start living together they have to share limited space, food, water, shelter, opposite sex partner, etc. This brings an intense competition among group members that may lead to the disorganization of the group. However, to cope with this, social animals have developed various kinds of mechanisms for avoidance of this competition. The dominance hierarchy is one of them, but not the only one. It was observed that one animal may allow other animal to eat, sleep and make contact with it, if the second animal is a grooming partner, coalition partner, consort partner or a playmate. The latter four types of behaviors are basic for the development of cooperative relationship and indirectly help in its maintenance.

Some direct ways of maintaining peace in the group are cooperative attack, cooperative defence and assuaging behavior. The aggression of some member(s) on the other member(s) is met with cooperative attack. On such occasions, two or more members may attack even the most dominant individual. In some cases, other individuals come to cooperatively defend the suffering monkey. Finally, members reciprocate among themselves their sufferings and needs that maintain the bonds of affection within the group.

Socio-biology of Cooperation, Help and Altruism

Earlier attempts to explain the evolution of altruism by the biologists were unsuccessful. A major theoretical formulation was, however, provided by Hamilton (1964). He proved that the social behaviour of a species evolves in such a way that the individual seems to value his neighbour's survival against his own according to the coefficient of relationship, that is, the fraction of genes shared by them. In the following years Hamilton's genetical kinship theory has undergone extensive research work in almost all branches of sciences engaged with the problem of evolution of social behaviour. Another predictive genetic model of mutualistic behaviour argues that in cases where aid is given, at some cost, the behaviour is reciprocally induced. The third type of genetic models of cooperation, help and altruism are based on group selection hypothesis. Group selection refers to a process of genetic change caused by differential extinction and proliferation of a group. The older notions of biological adaptations, e.g., for the good of the group or species are no more valid. Lastly, some genetic models of helping behaviour borrow game theory from social sciences.

The genetic viewpoint of helping behaviour is controvertial in case of primates. Several social scientists and biologists suggest the role of cultural transmission and learning processes; both individual and social. For example, the recognition of close relatives, essential for kin selection theory, may involve both learning and genetic components. Besides that it may also need development of considerable cognitive skills among the group members.

Group Dynamics

An important area where interaction is possible between social psychologists and socio-biologists is the study of group dynamics. Theories developed by social psychologists in this area can be tested on or applied to the study of the groups of nonhuman primates. There was a time when psychologists considered 'individual' as real and 'group' was considered as mystical. Through his field studies and laboratory experiments on humans, Curt Lewin made the psychologists accept the notion that group *per se* have characteristics and the behaviour of an individual is greatly influenced by the group to which he belongs (Lewin, 1948). In recent years the applied value of group concept can be seen in the 'tragedy of commons' where the short-term self-serving benefits create long-term mutual cost (Hardins, 1968). One must understand how and when to sacrifice short-term individual gains, in the interest of long-term mutual gain. This is a problem of interdependence among group members, known as the 'social trap' (Cross & Guyer, 1980) that manifests itself in various forms, e.g., depletion of resources, extinction of various species, water and air pollution, etc.

According to Lewin, the group is the dynamic whole or the Gestalt. It must be understood in terms of causal relationships among its members. One of his key concepts in describing and analyzing groups is cohesiveness. This refers to all forces which bind the parts of group together and which resist disruption. We can borrow from Gestalt psychologists the principles of perceptual organisation. These principles were originally propounded to study the perception of homogeniety in physical phenomena. However, these are general principles concerning the conditions conducive to the perception of the collection of individuals or units as parts of a higher system. The units or elements organize in the mind if: (*a*) they are in proximity, i.e., temporal or spatial closeness; (*b*) there is qualitative or quantitative similarity, i.e., same colour, same size, etc. (*c*) they have a common boundary; (*d*) they have common fate, i.e., move together (*e*) past experience or custom has led to similar responses to various elements; and (*f*) expectation or set that the elements are to be grouped together (Box 5.2).

The essence of group is the interdependence of its members, which varies in degree from loose mass to compact unit. Deutsch (1973) indicated that the interdependence is that of promotive or cooperative interdependence rather than contrient or competitive interdependence. Deutsch made it clear that group cohesiveness is the average of the various individuals' chioces to remain in group.

To study the nature of mutual interdependence among members of a group, we have examined Deutsch's hypotheses. The positive cathexis hypothesis predicts that members of a cooperative group develop affectionate relationships among each other. Social grooming is one of the most widely accepted affectionate relationship in monkeys. Thus we asked, do the macaques and langurs differ in social grooming? The positive inducibility hypothesis helps us to predict that members in cohesive group are more likely to give and solicit support from each other.

Box 5.2: Gestalt principles of organisation

A GROUP WILL REMAIN AS A UNIT, UNTIL,

COHESIVE FORCES > or = DISUNIFYING FORCES
(cooperative) (competitive)

BASIC PRINCIPLES: ELEMENTS EMERGE AS A GROUP IF THEY HAVE FOLLOWING QUALITIES

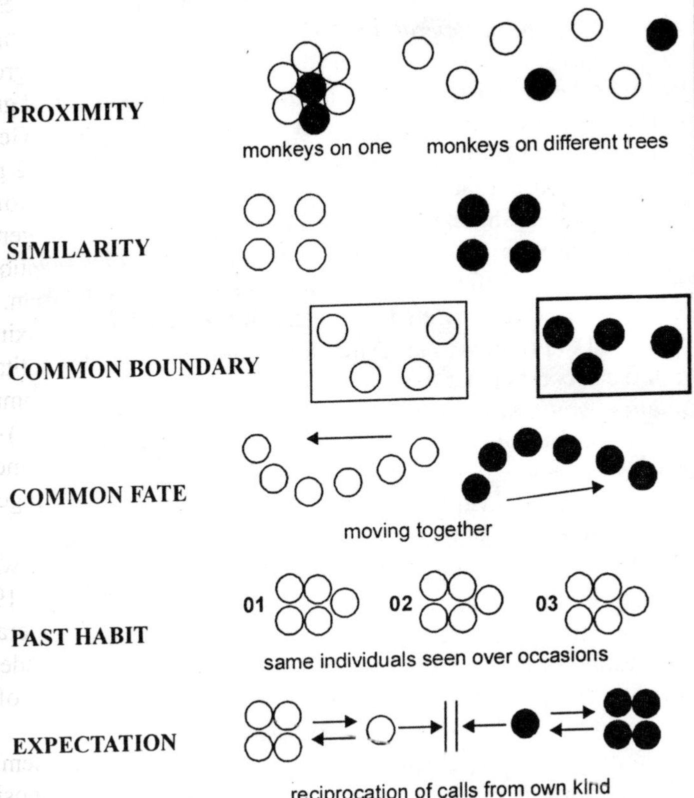

Fight interference is a very conspicuous cooperative behavior found in monkeys where support is given to conspecifics. We tried to

find if the macaques and langurs differ in cooperative attack and cooperative defence? According to substitutability hypothesis participation in cooperative activities leads to the division of labour and consequently role assignment. Therefore we were interested to know, do the macaques and langurs differ in role differentiation?

Crook (1970) has even earlier pointed out that one approach in social sciences that failed to make impact was poineered long back by Kropotkin and later by Allee, is the role of mutual assistance in the evolution of social systems. He suggested that much complex cooperative behavior appears to involve the resolution of social tensions so that breakdown is prevented.

Urbanisation and Cooperation

The eminent ethologist, Tinbergen (1976) has emphasised that various 'psycho-social pressures' arising from new social circumstances may cause several types of 'psychosomatic disorders': duodenal ulcers, forms of asthma, coronary thrombosis and heart disease, hypertension, etc. One potential strategy to understand this problem can be to collect information from detailed studies of healthy as compared to unhealthy consequences of different living conditions for some primates, that are at the same time related to us and in their social organisation convergent to primitive man. After describing various changes going on in the urban populations, he pointed out "*While life in primitive societies, and undoubtedly in our ancestral in-group, required a balanced mixture of competition and cooperation, many circumstances seem now combine to reward over-competitiveness.*"

The solution to this is to gain knowledge on the biological forerunners of cooperation, by observing different species in their natural environments, e.g., the present study on rhesus monkeys. This will help in formulating principles, for the society, in which mutual support is more valued. According to Harlow and Harlow (1966), "*The evolution of the potentialities for forming strong affectional bonds must have played a role in the success of the primate order in the development of adaptable social organisations. With positive ties within and between age ranges, the group could cohere, permitting animals relatively weak and poorly designed for individual defence to act cooperatively to hold predators at check.*"

The following study filled this gap in order to have a wider understanding of cooperative nature of the group. Our attempt was to answer the question: *has the urban environment affected the quality and quantity of cooperative behaviour in rhesus macaques and langurs?* At Shimla there was an ideal situation to conduct comparative study on the behaviour of macaques and langurs living sympatrically in urban and forest habitat. The following section briefly present our findings on cooperative behaviour in macaques and langurs to understand the nature of mutual interdependence in a primate group.

The langurs and macaques differ significantly on six cooperative behaviours. Rhesus monkeys move more cooperatively than the langurs. These monkeys defend their group members from external threats to a much greater degree than the langurs. Within the group rhesus monkeys are more friendly than langurs: the macaques groom each other more than the langurs; and the rhesus monkeys interfere within group fights more often than the langurs (by participating in cooperative attack and cooperative defence). The young and infant langurs engage more in social play than the rhesus monkeys. There is similarity in various other ways of cooperative life in langurs and macaques. Both kinds of monkeys show age-sex class differences in expressing various care-giving and care-eliciting behaviours (Figure 5.2).

The role of culture, socialisation practices and other environmental influences on pro-social behavior in humans is alluring psychologists. A meta-analytic study concludes that country people are more helpful than city people. Can this conclusion be generalised to nonhuman primates? Comparative studies on the behaviour of nonhuman primates living in urban and forest areas are rare (Roonwal, 1976). After extensive field and laboratory studies, Singh (1969) concludes that in comparison to forest monkeys, urban monkeys are more aggressive, more curious, more exploratory but equal in learning ability.

In the present study the environment turned out to be an important variable which significantly affected cooperative movement, cooperative foraging, communal attack and social grooming. As expected, cooperative movement and cooperative foraging decreased in the urban area, whereas, communal attack and social grooming increased in the urban area. The urban environment did not affect communal defence, assuaging behavior, cooperative defence, cooperative attack and social play.

Fig. 5.2: Role differentiation in the rhesus monkey and the Hanuman langur (N=17 for each species; principal component analysis of scores on 40 behavior categories for each subject)

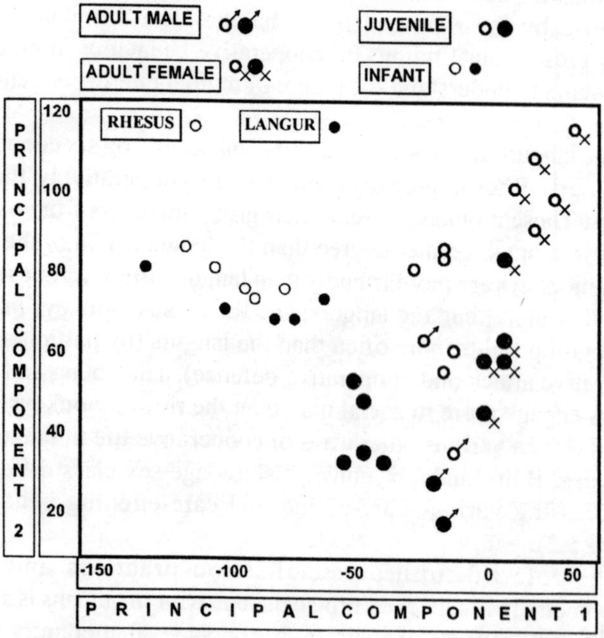

There was highly significant interaction between species and environment for communal attack as well as social grooming (Figure 5.3). It was found that communal attack and social grooming increased in the urban area in case of rhesus monkeys only. Among langurs the two behaviors remained similar in the urban as well as forest environment. This is a highly significant finding and shows how urban environment affects the two species, differently.

Grooming is the major cooperative behaviour in both urban and forest monkeys. Soon after the birth of an infant, the mother starts grooming it. The infant starts reciprocating it towards the end of his first year that continuously increases, if the infant is a female, but decreases after juvenile age, if it is a male. Grooming not only serves the function of body cleaning, but it is also the regulator of social relationships.

Fig. 5.3: Social grooming is greater among urban rhesus monkeys

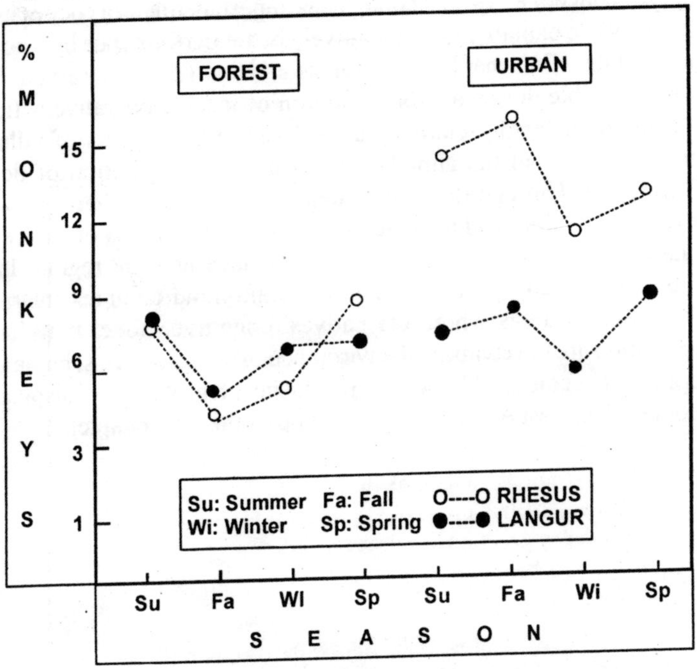

The studies on cooperative interdependence in primate groups along with the co-evolutionary approach of Gadgil (Chapter 4) have been combined with the vision of sustainable development observed among people of Himalayas, which has much wider application to understand the nature and society relationship. The main points of the natives' cognitive model as articulated by the present investigator are presented in the next chapter.

The native people of the Himalayas perceive development from a holistic point of view (Pirta, 2001). In such a paradigm, the development of both the individual and community are important. For the normal functioning of the individual, head (knowledge), heart (compassion) and hands (actions) must function in harmony with one another during the mundane day-to-day activities and to achieve self-enlightenment, the ultimate goal. At the community level, 'humanitarian' scientists, compassionate poets and writers, and social workers should work towards the attainment of welfare of the humanity.

In this integrative approach, besides ideas, people are the major focus of concern and social context has important role in a cooperative action. While explaining comparatively better performance by a north Indian state, Himachal Pradesh, Dreze and Sen (2002) observed that it was possible due to a strong tradition of local cooperative action. An important factor, relatively unexplored in the context of village social structure in the Himalayan region is the institution of deity (Chapter 7). Through these local deities, the primitive heroes come alive from folklore and mediate the development and maintenance of cohesiveness among the people of the village and the region. It is here that the ecology, culture and the brain-mind complex interact. The different areas where the natives' cognitive model may have application are the creation of environmental consciousness, humanist approach to ecological issues and mental health problems of displaced people. These issues have been taken up in the next chapter.

6

Native Wisdom

Human social conflicts have evolutionary as well as cultural past. However, changes in inner and outer contextual features drastically affect the nature of conflicts and their resolution. A conflict arises when two activities are incompatible. It may occur within the individual, which is termed as intra-psychic conflict. But more important for us here are conflicts originating due to incompatible cognitions of two or more groups. The resolution of these social conflicts depends on the consonance among the cognitive beliefs. Consider the following examples.

When India was facing the challenge of its survival and was in turmoil due to social conflicts, Sri Aurobindo envisaged the union of all streams so that "*one mighty river, one purifying and redeeming Ganges, pour it over the death-in-life of a materialistic humanity as Bhagiratha led down the Ganges and flooded with it the ashes of his fathers, so that there may be a resurrection of the soul in mankind and the Satyayuga for a while return to the world.*" (SABCL Vol. 16, p. 430)

There is yet another important dimension which includes conflicts between individual and collective interests. They are called 'social dilemmas' or 'social traps.' Our social problems generally include conflicts between individual and collective preferences embedded in the environmental milieu. An ecologist, Madhav Gadgil, has explored social conflicts along this dimension in the institution of local deity in the villages, "*One often finds associated with such deities a rich body of folklore which can illuminate the history of human groups that worship these deities. Such folklore can be particularly fascinating when it appears to have its origin in conflicts of interests amongst the different human groups.*" (Gadgil, 2001; p. 164). These two perspectives, the first by a philosopher and the second by an ecologist, are important for us to understand the conflicts involving people in the villages of India.

Human social conflicts have a very significant dimension, they are entrenched in the culture. The western material culture grew in the modern cities while in contrast the Indian culture has its origins in small village communities in the forests. The material science would therefore be of little use to the villages of India, where most of its people live, unless it was assimilated by the indigenous culture. This was a point of discord, between Gandhi and Nehru (Mitrany[1]) at the time of independence of India. However more important is the premise of the famous poet Rabindranath Thakur (1986) that the origin of culture in the forest was the uniqueness of the land known as *Bharatavarsha.* The isolation in dense forests made people turn their minds inward in search of the infinite mysteries of the world. This inward quest is peculiarly a method of acquisition of knowledge among people who made their discoveries in the *tapovans*.

In the first half of the twentieth century, Mahatma Gandhi successfully tested an ancient discovery "the law of nonviolence" by his inward quest (Pyarelal, 1959). The use of non-resistance as a device to resolve conflict has some validation in the naturalistic observations of Kropotkin (1914) and Lorenz (1976) well known for exploring the laws of jungle for maintaining peace in animal societies.[2] For the social scientists in India there is a lot more to explore in Gandhi's unusual experiments, as the famous psychologist Bandura (2001) saw in non-violence for enhancing self-efficacy.

Whether the theory of the "idiocy of village life" in India carries any weight is a contentious issue. However, for the noted historian, Kosambi, the self-contained village provided "*the material foundation for Indian culture and civilization*" (Kosambi, 1975). He felt that the Indian society has developed more by successive religious transformations (and associated philosophical developments) than by violence. It was, however, saddening that the study of primitive village deities evoked superficial interest among social scientists. Kosambi observed that it needed much deeper analysis.

People of India have a spiritual affinity with the river Ganges, the legendary Bhagirathi. And their association with the Himalaya is numinous as well. But, over the past several decades, the Ganga and the Himalaya are facing the onslaught of domineering policies in the name of human development. The effects of these activities may be seen in non-living as well as living beings. In the latter case the affected person is more likely to be a native of the Himalayas but a greater concern from a distant person is possible. This is noteworthy in the opinion of thinker Vidyanivas Misra (Box 6.1). For him, the important question was not, to whom the Ganga belonged instead more significant was who belonged to the Ganga (Misra, 1995a). In order to be of the Ganga, it was not the material ownership that had a bearing but it was the assimilation of the Ganga's rich cultural identity, and the determination of our own identity from the Ganga (Misra, 1995b). In this he has probably resolved the dilemma of some social scientists (G. Misra & Gergen, 2001) while introducing the concept of cultural relativism.

Box 6.1: The role of media

After a ban on the felling of trees in the Himalayas in 1983 (Appendix 1), there was a proposal to review the situation after ten years. Therefore in 1993 a suggestion had come from the forest departments in the respective Himalayan states to start felling of trees on scientific basis. In a desperate effort some Chipko activists, already entrenched in the anti-Tehri Dam movement, met the authorities. Meeting was held and an appeal was made to continue ban on the felling of trees in the Himalaya. It had no effect.

Fortunately, a young journalist from Shimla was keeping track of the working plans being made by the Forest Department in Himachal Pradesh to start the felling in the garb of the 'scientific forestry'. He along with our appeal made a strong plea for the proposed disastrous action. This was the first page news in the *Times of India* (Hindi Edition) with the editorial by Misra. The effect was sudden and strong. All plans of felling trees in the Himalayas were shelved.

One way suggested to achieve the cultural relativism was through the grass-roots resistance or movements. Strangely, the suggestion came from two opposite streams, one was an American social psychologist Kenneth Gergen[3] and the other an Indian thinker Misra (1995b). This solution to resolve the social issues was not different from the affirmative action of social workers, taken in the 1970s in the Western Himalayas, about which we are talking in this chapter.

In order to comprehend the spirit of this social movement, we may have to visualize the social scenario in the western Himalaya during the last century. For long, the forest policies have been a matter of dispute in the western Himalayan region as they strained the relationship of local people with their forests. Now there is good amount of evidence in several well researched theses about the degeneration of West Himalayan forests during the British rule (Chhatre, 2003; Singh, 1998). Dangwal (2005) writes that the, "*State control over forests was strengthened when they were reserved after the passing of the Forest Acts in 1865 and 1878. The forest department now systematically surveyed the forests and made them accessible for the large-scale timber operations. The extraction of wood grew rapidly in the late 19th century and the process continued till the early 1920s. For a decade, the timber market slumped; first due to the post-war crash of timber and then due to the Great Economic Depression. The scale of wood extraction reached new heights during the Second World War*." He further mentioned that forests were overexploited in Uttarakhand (now Uttaranchal state) even after the independence.

The conflict reached to such an extent by the 1970s that, where on one hand the forests in their vicinities became almost inaccessible to the poor local folks, on the other hand a few wealthy contractors of the plains could lay their hands on the forest produce of their choice. The scale of this denudation of the Himalaya by the contractors, facilitated by the government policies, was so enormous that the landscape was turning brown.

Perceiving the helplessness of the local people and the blind eye of the government towards the cordiality of the natives to forests, the deeply wounded folk poet could foresee the nature of events. His insightful solution for the impending threat on the lives of trees and local folks came out in a poem at midnight. The message of the poem was very clear, there was a call for a collective action "*Hug the trees, don't let them being cut*." These words of the folk poet Ghanshayam Sailani in 1972, in a period of social turmoil, touched the hearts of people. The following years, it seemed, were destined to witness the Chipko (hug the trees) in action, which the poet later declared as "the War of Dharma." In this way, an apparently selfish struggle for survival, after getting embedded in the indigenous spiritual context, took a new turn. This was an unusual socio-cognitive invention of people's non-violent struggle in the Himalayas.

In their pursuit to search universal laws of behavior, social scientists are indifferent to flourishing societies and cultures in diverse terrain. As a consequence of this, the public image of social sciences remains a mirage (Misra & Gergen, 2002; Segall, Dasen, Berry & Poortinga, 1999; WHO, 2001). These contextual variables, for instance, are important as they provide 'developmental niche' for a child or have significance in creating antecedent conditions for harmony and conflict in the groups. The following account provides glimpses of the environmental conflicts between natives of the Western Himalayas and the proponents of modern development.

The legendary Bhagirathi, the Ganga, has an integral association with the body and the soul of Indians. They also cherish a similar relationship with the Himalayas. In recent years, the Ganga and the Himalaya have been facing the invasion of economic development policies. As a result of this the very nature of the Himalaya and the Ganga has been changing physically as well as in the psyche of Indians. The consequences of such changes will have detrimental effects, not only on our vision of the revered mountains and rivers, but also on our cultural heritage. It may also prove to be a threat to the survival of human beings. Those interventions have some correlation with shrinking of forest cover, drying of water sources, increase in soil erosion, receding glaciers and scarcity of medicinal plants. We have failed to reverse these trends. Thus, on one hand the dynamic balance among the components of the ecosystem is changing and on the other hand it has an intrinsic relation with the overall development of people living in those mountainous regions.

For instance, the construction of the large dams in the Himalayas has raised several important issues in the recent past, particularly the rehabilitation of ousted people has become a significant humanitarian problem. In India, since 1950, the big dams have usurped a significant proportion of land belonging to the highlanders of the river valleys of the western Himalayas (Bahuguna, 1978; Bhatt, 1992; Valdiya, 1992). This situation is aggravated due to an apathetic attitude towards the social and psychological trauma faced by the ousted people. Nonetheless, the construction of large dams is going on in total disregard for the aspirations of the native people, virtually making a mockery of the holistic approach to development. Unfortunately, the technocrats look to maximize profits accruing from the megawatts of hydroelectric power. In this process millions of 'developmental refugees' have been created by large dams, as a result people have become averse to such kind of development.

Contemporary thinkers of India (Chaitanya, 2000; Chidananda, 1987; Dharampal, 1993; Misra, 1994; Thakar, 1989) point out that the mysterious East has a potential to contribute in various fields of psychology, non-material as well as material, but it is not interesting enough for psychologists in India. It is a matter of great concern that the latter have even neglected the environmental issues troubling people. For example, issues such as displacement, rehabilitation and aversive attitude towards big dams are not important for social scientists in India. The process of development has various aspects that can be evaluated in the context of the well-being of people. For India, 'much of the task that Nehru had identified remains largely unaccomplished' (Sen, 1997) if we consider the *constitutive* elements of well-being rather than the *utilitarian* elements. They signify a 'mental state' view and the 'desire-fulfillment' respectively (Sen, 1999).

The thinking of the environmentalists is converging on a point that the wrong developmental paradigm in third world countries, like India, create situations of inequality and exploitation that lead to frustration and rebellion among people (Gadgil & Guha, 1995). Speaking '*of the more holistic or comprehensive cognition of those at the receiving end of the present world system*' Nandy (1998) warns about new forms of violence and injustice in concepts such as development, growth, history, science and technology. They may be used as tools of oppression within the same region and at the hands of people within. Studies relating to natives of Garhwal and Kumaon in the Western Himalayas (Bora, 1996; Hoon, 1996), where two large dams are coming up, point to the hollowness of the policies of development.

But a lot more disturbing is a misconception in the minds of materialists that the social relations follow the same laws as particles of matter. The fault partly lies with social scientists, who in order to give their discipline the hue of a science, borrowed materialist principles and methods (Bandyopadhay, 2001). It is also true that the physical scientists and the technocrats, being individuals living in a society, develop a false sense of complacence that they understand social phenomena. They, however, dilute the very nature of the social concepts (Sen, 1995). Behavioural scientists must make physical scientists realize that displacement and rehabilitation involve social and psychological factors and thus the technical solution is not the sole issue. The emphasis on material is not enough (Varadarajan, 1998) and therefore psychological factors need incorporation in the economic paradigm (Sen, 1997). For instance, people in general adapt physically to environmental changes, but psychologically they are likely to face problems. Perhaps this is true in case of displaced people who are apparently normal, but have strong feelings of disgruntlement with the whole system.

Ecological psychologists consider 'behaviour settings' as primary determinants of action. Today, these behaviour settings are insecure, yet many factors compel a fairly large number of citizens towards them. One such factor is the construction of large dams in the Himalayas and other parts of India, which is causing displacement of people from their native habitat. Ousted people live in behaviour settings that are impoverished in comparison to their native habitats and in settings that expose them to a whole set of unknown dangers. When people come in contact with the dominant culture, the acculturation starts, which is stressful. Ousted people, for various reasons, are prone to such stress. A large population of these people have accumulated since 1950s who have been displaced from their native habitats. In India, there are at least 20 million oustees of big dams and irrigation projects (Fernandes, Das & Rao, 1989; Roy, 1999). The breakdown of social support system and the separation from loved objects also occurs during the process of displacement due to large dams. These two factors, along with acculturation have probably negative effects on the mental health of displaced people.

Historically, in the mountains, people have settled along river valleys. A rich diversity of culture sprouted along these rivers and adjacent mountain landscape (Singh, 1998). Nonetheless, the modern policy of development with an attendant strong drive to harness natural resources of the Himalaya, for example forests for timber and rivers for hydroelectricity, is heading for a civilization's collapse. It involves denudation of hill slopes and inundation of living habitat. Since independence, a large-scale intensification of these two 'developmental activities' has been taking place in the Western Himalayas, while planners show scant regard for an integrated vision of life. All this has been going on in total disregard to the aspirations of native people. This situation is aggravated due to an apathetic attitude towards the social and psychological trauma and injustice faced by the native people.

The above description presents a grim scenario of the developmental paradigm in the Western Himalayas. It is based on an incorrect understanding that social relations are physical relations, coupled with insecure behaviour settings, accculturative stress, and breakdown of social support system, which negatively affects social and psychological well-being of people. The natives of Garhwal, in the Western Himalayas, experienced these negative consequences, which provoked them against these developmental processes. The natives perceived these processes unsustainable because it exhausted natural resources, made livelihood miserable and threatened future generations. The first move of natives was to resist logging operations denuding the green cover from hill slopes, followed by a struggle against the large-scale technological interventions in the Himalayas symbolized by big dams. During these struggles, the environmental consciousness of native people gradually crystallized into a holistic approach to development that has been articulated here in the form of a cognitive model.

It would be appropriate to assess the importance of this folk wisdom in context of the drawbacks in the theoretical orientations that have been dicussed in Chapter 4. The native model presented here has relevance for the resolution of environmental conflicts in the Indian context. In the preceding chapter we provided evidence on the cooperative life in primate groups from the naturalistic studies on non-human primate species. This has significance because the models presented about the nature of human group assume that altruistic and co-operative behaviour cannot evolve in social groups. The primary interactions taking place within the group members are basically selfish in nature. Note particularly the stance taken by an economist, Anup Shah (1998) in Chapter 4 about feasibility of cooperative interactions. However these are some exceptions.

For example, it is important to note the observations of Dreze and Sen (2002) in *India: Development and Participation*, on co-operative action and social context. They have suggested that, "*social development in Himachal Pradesh (and also, to varying extents, in other parts of the Himalayan region) has been facilitated by a relatively favourable social context, which includes the comparative lack of sharp social disparities in village communities and a strong tradition of local co-operative action.*" (Dreze & Sen, 2002; p. 179). These economists have analyzed various factors conducive to development in Himachal Pradesh, however, they did not report those institutions which promote the cooperative action.

In the present volume we describe a success story of the cooperative action guided by folk wisdom. It is well recognized in saving the forest of the Himalayas and other parts of India. This success story is analysed in this chapter of the report. We also suggest that the role of the institutions of local deity in keeping the hill society together has remained almost unnoticed.

There are some important questions that we have to answer. We must find out how to arrive at non-coercive solutions to environmental problems. At the same time we have to search ways, how short-term individual interests can be sacrificed in favour of long-term common interests. However, the most important question is how to elicit voluntary participation of communities with conflicting interests in pro-environmental activities. Perhaps the people of Himalayas have answered these questions in their own way. The main objective of this chapter is to present their views as a holistic paradigm of development. The following part of the chapter has four sections: first we give an overview of the Chipko Movement. The second section is articulation of the natives' cognition of development by the present investigator. A brief discussion of the implications of the model for the social sciences in general is given in the third section. The last section provides evidence on the application of natives' cognitive model for resolving environmental issues.

An Overview of the Chipko Movement

Natives of the Garhwal Himalayas became aware of mounting ecological crisis in the Himalayas several decades ago. In the 1970s some voluntary social workers picked up strands from the cultural heritage of India and neatly wove a grass-roots environmental campaign known as the Chipko—hug-the-tree—movement (Bahuguna, 1974; Kunwar, 1982; Sarala Devi, 1980). The Chipko Movement has its origins in the environmental context of the Garhwal Himalayas, which was characterized by large scale logging operations managed by private contractors. The peasants from remote villages of the Western Himalayas rose in peaceful revolt against government's logging policies that interfered with the calm but already hard life of the hill folk. The Man of the Trees, Richard St. Barbe Baker (1982) was the first person who paid tribute to thousands of Garhwali men and women by visiting their far-flung villages.

The natives of the Garhwal Himalaya followed a non-violent method of resistance to government's policies that flouted basic principles of their cognized model of development. The first phase of the environment movement, devoted to protect the Himalayan forests, continued from the 1970s to the 1990s. During this period social workers of Chipko not only created an environmental consciousness but also convinced the government to make a drastic change in its forest policy. As a result, the government of India announced ten-year moratorium on felling of green trees in the Himalaya in 1983, which was partially reviewed in 1993, but the ban has continued (Appendix 1). After that, the natives started a new struggle to save the whole mountain ecosystem of the Himalaya in the form of a broad based Himalaya Bachao Andolan (Save Himalaya Movement; Appendix 2). This movement focussed its energy to prevent the construction of the Tehri Dam and to mobilize public opinion in favour of small hydroelectric projects (Pirta, 2001). While some social workers in the Henwal Ghati, who had participated in Chipko, have chosen to save the traditional varieties of crops grown in the Himalayan region (Prasun, 1996), the others in Chamba in Himachal Pradesh and Gopeshwar and Kumaon in Uttaranchal are, however, continuing their efforts to save green cover of the hills.

The Chipko Movement has attracted the attention of social scientists from all over the world. One after the other, several intellectuals have climbed the hills of the Garhwal Himalaya and have come back with different versions of the Chipko (Berreman, 1989; Guha, 1989; Rangan, 2001; Shiva & Bandyopadhyay, 1986; Weber, 1988). There should be no doubt about the academic excellence of those stories, but it is unlikely that such stories help in the real cause, the 'development' of the native people. Although the writers of those stories became 'renowned environmentalists' (for a self-appraisal see Rangan, 2001), while the people still remain "natives" for them, yet they are not able to comprehend their analytic finesse. This raises a second and perhaps more relevant question. Are we really trying to understand the viewpoint of the native people? Those academic storytellers have analyzed the role of natives with the *untested* propositions of X's, Y's and Z's in the West. The natives, however, have at least tested their propositions.

The following section describes this indigenous approach to the development, which originated during native people's struggle to save the Himalayas. In natives' approach there is an awareness of the sustainability of life that besides the physical encompasses its social, psychological and spiritual aspects, which are deep-rooted in the Hindu world-view.

The Natives' Cognition of Sustainable Development

The native people of the Garhwal Himalaya perceive developmental process from holistic point of view (Pirta, 2003, 04; Figure 6.1). In such a paradigm, the development of the individual as well as the community is important. For the normal functioning of the individual his head (knowledge), heart (compassion) and hands (actions) must function in harmony with one another during the mundane day to day activities and to achieve self-enlightenment, the ultimate goal. In this way one has to acquire, for example, such information, as that oak trees are suitable for the Himalayan ecosystem. After this one has to plant the oak species in preference to other species when there is an occasion, and finally, he must empathize with oak trees for their better growth and protection. Mira Behn was an embodiment of such knowledge, action and devotion. She was the one who perceived a link between the oak (*banj*) tree, the Himalayan ecosystem and the overall well being of hill people. She has also been a source of inspiration for the natives of the Garhwal Himalaya.

At the community level 'humanitarian' scientists, compassionate poets and writers, and social workers should work towards the attainment of welfare of all, living and non-living. Sarala Devi, another disciple of Gandhi Ji, sacrificed her life for the people of the Himalayas. She had been running a school for girls and also initiated Sarvodaya workers in pro-environmental actions. Those Sarvodaya workers were later the forerunners of the Chipko Movement. They followed a holistic developmental approach and paid special attention to the cause of the poor section of the society. For instance, "*Bimla Behin and her husband Sunderlal Bahuguna, it will be remembered, chose to set up their ashram in the Simiyana valley because of the high concentration of harijans in that area.*" (Alter, 2002; p. 122).

The native's cognition of development reminds modern man that his 'material development' is a path towards *vikriti* (destruction). That this is not intended to be a form of escapism should be clear from the call of Swami Chidananda (1987), a *sanyasin* and a patron of the Chipko Movement: "*We have to wake ourselves up and save the Himalayas and the Ganges.*" Chidananda (1991) explains that *Prakriti* has a dualistic nature. As a principle it afflicts *Purusha*, and *Yoga* has been especially developed to separate *Purusha* from *Prakriti*. But the world all around us, with which we interact and feel happiness and sorrow, is also *Prakriti*, the mother who sustains us all. Indeed in this world, which is a manifestation of *Prakriti*, each person has to follow an order that sustains life (*dharma*), pursue some economic activity or transaction for day to day living (*artha*), participate in procreation (*kama*), and, work for attainment of salvation (*moksha*).

Fig. 6.1: The natives' cognitive model of sustainable development

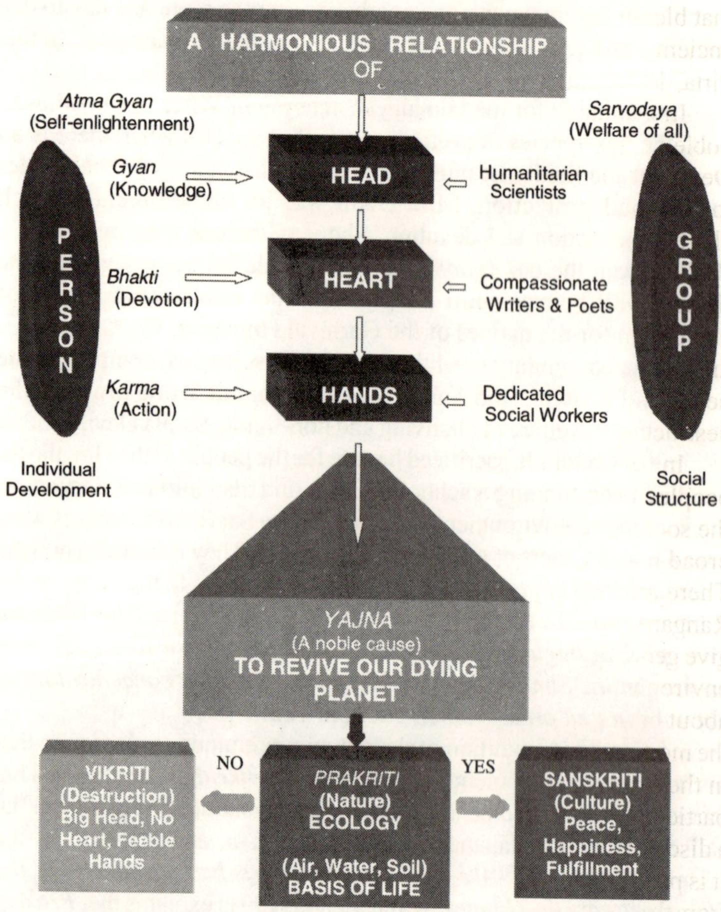

The wisdom of the people of Himalayas is that air, water and soil are the main products of forest whereas for a silviculturist, forest is for timber. For the people of the Himalayas, believing means doing. It

aptly describes the method of the Chipko social worker in creating environmental awareness. For example, the Chipko activist would show to the rural masses slides of the denuded countryside in the hills, of the depleted water sources, fodder scarcity, soil erosion, the floods in the rivers, etc. to explain the negative consequences of the forest destruction. Those images are supplemented by a commentary that blends the information from scientific studies and the wisdom of ancient Indian traditions (Bahuguna, 1982; Bandyopadhayay, 1992; Pirta, 1994, 2000; Tikekar, 1988).

In such a paradigm, everybody has to engage in the *yajna*, the noble cause, of preserving the nature's balance on our planet (Sarala Devi, 1982). The native of the Himalayas says 'Yes' to life and 'No' to death while following the way towards culture, *sanskriti*, which is characterized by qualities such as peace, happiness and fulfillment (Bahuguna, 1997). The native people of the Himalayas are against those values, which regard nature as a commodity to be used or exploited by human beings. Where a person competes for materialistic knowledge (big head), he has no compassion for fellow beings (no heart) and he avoids manual work (feeble hands). It is a path towards destruction, *vikriti*, in contrast to culture, *sanskriti*.

In the above section I have presented the cognitive model of the people of Himalayas on the sustainable development, familiar among the social scientists as the Chipko, which has now transformed into a broad based Himalaya Bachao Andolan (Save Himalaya Movement). There are excellent alternate sources (Berreman, 1989; Guha, 1989; Rangan, 2001; Shiva & Bandyopadhyay, 1986; Weber, 1988), which give general information and provide extensive analyses of this pioneer environmental movement of India. One must, however, be careful about biases of those analysts regarding the social issues taken up by the movement and the actors involved in it. The picture I have presented in the above section is by a person who is a native of the Himalaya, a participant and a psychologist at the same time. Therefore, first of all a disclaimer, it is *not* a selective, an authoritative, and the final account. It is presented here with a view that the movement has still far escaped from the scrutiny of psychologists. This is necessary because in essence the movement has deeper psychological ramifications. More important, however, is the potential of the holistic approach of this movement as an indigenous paradigm in environmental psychology. This would require its application in understanding environmental issues so that we can modify and evolve it.

In the model of sustainable development presented above, some concepts have been used that need further explanation if the model is to be related to social sciences in general. The following section deals with this issue. My attempt here is to suggest some broad relationships between the native's cognition and apparently similar issues of behavioral scientists.

Socio-psychological Implications of the Model

The human race is a highly unique constituent of the ecosystem excelling in its ability to cognize the environment and to make the environment suitable for itself. The aim of environmental psychology is to understand these dynamic relationships of human beings with their surroundings. As a method, reductionism is central to the discipline of psychology, however, the holistic paradigm is gaining recognition in the area of environmental psychology. This change has special importance for us in India, perhaps because "*The Hindu mind is essentially synthetic. It always analyses a problem into its various aspects, and considers them in their synthetic relation to one another*." (Sinha, 1958, p. xvii). In this way the holistic paradigm can be an important link for the exchange of ideas between the East and the West on various global environmental problems.

In recent years, at least two points of convergence are visible between the East and the West in the area of environment. One of them is the realization that there is need for a radical change in human relationship with nature. For this new relationship with nature a holistic approach is imperative that is partly religious in temperament (Chaitanya, 2000) and is open to native wisdom of primal societies (Goldsmith, 1998). The Deep Ecology (Naess, 1989) is also a meeting point for the East and the West. But the other most significant area of convergence is emerging from the scientific acceptability of holistic relationships, which presently can be seen in the case of Gaia Hypothesis (Bunyard, 1996; Lovelock, 1979). Gaia is an all encompassing whole of the planet earth and its atmosphere. The Indian tradition has the concept of Mother Earth, *dharati mata*, since ages (Tripathi, 2002), and the people of India relate with her in multitudinous ways. We may have to develop a new vocabulary to describe the holistic relationships, because science customarily uses fragmentary language to narrate these phenomena of nature. As far as native-nonnative distinction is concerned it is the reflection of a person's response to physical and social environmental features and also related to his personality attributes (Ittelson, Proshansky, Rivlin & Winkel, 1974).

Spiritual thinkers as well as psychologists hypothesize the concept of an internal state of harmony, however, its attributes are seldom made clear. For spiritualists like Krishnamurti (2000), the harmony of mind/brain, heart and body is a state of intelligence that is not governed by space, time and other physical measures. His book *The Awakening of Intelligence* is a rational dialogue on this harmonious relationship. It has a survival function. We want to avoid 'uncertainty' and seek 'order.' As from the viewpoint of psychologists (Dalal, 2001), they also try to understand the integration of thinking, mood (emotion) and behaviour. For example, mental and behavioural disorders are conceived as alterations in these three components accompanied with personal distress and/or impaired functioning.

The native's model presented here may have some similarity with the models of Gestalt social psychologists such as Heider and Festinger (Rock & Palmer, 1990). Heider in his principle of balance proposes that individuals prefer harmonious cognitive relations. On similar lines, Festinger's cognitive dissonance model hypothesizes that people seek to reduce inconsistencies in their beliefs, feelings and behaviour. Gestalt psychologists opine that we are taking interest in environmental psychology due to a feeling of suffocation in our urban environment and therefore we are now searching ways to live in harmony with nature (Ittelson et al., 1974).

Let us now consider two examples exploring the possibility of the development of models based on within and between harmonious social relationships from two important sectors, the management and the labour. The prime reason suggested for these alternative models is the ineffectiveness of the materialist model of development in certain Eastern cultures. These investigators have independently found that the harmony of thoughts, feelings and actions is important in a variety of interdependent relationships in organizations as has already been suggested in the native cognitive model of sustainable development.

It is a strange coincidence that the two studies mentioned here, independently report, about the importance of a harmonious state in social relations. A study on managers reports that the harmony of *gyan*, *bhakti* and *karma* is a characteristic of cultures that form the southern Asia cluster. Investigators of a project, the GLOBE, have observed that the model of management based on capitalist economics has limited value for organizations in south Asia (Gupta, Surie, Javidan & Chhokar, 2002). They, however, believe that southern Asian managers are likely to adopt integrative value-based approach that is rooted in the regional philosophy, which has maintained deep interaction among the three core concepts of knowledge, devotion and action.

The second study compares two scenarios of the ontology of labor in the north eastern region of India. In stark contrast to the mainstream capitalist ontology of labor prevalent in most parts of India, the scenario in the north eastern region, as depicted in the study (Batola, 2003) is: Human— Creative— Organic (Nature—Society)— Natural reproduction— Sustainable— Community and family labour— Empowering— Harmonious. The modern economic development, however, has induced redundancies and obsolescence in the North-Eastern region instead of improving the quality and quantity of labor. Now imagine the state of affairs in a region where the percentage of total workers is higher than the percentage in the country.

Development needs to be aligned to values of society. While developing his argument on this line of thinking, Tripathi (2002) observes that developmental interventions can be more effective in India by incorporating existing values from the society. However, his cautionary note is, "*In suggesting that one way to align development to values is to look for a moral principle which will harmonize values in conflict, the idea is not to direct development in terms of religion but only to use religious and moral symbols to achieve a more open and integrated society.*" (Tripathi, 2002, p. 323) If our goal is 'sustainable development', which has been defined as the 'socially responsible development' by the Earth Summit 1992, then perhaps the need for a value based approach for human development is imperative.

It may be appropriate here to clarify the meaning of the holistic approach. We can proceed to understand the holistic approach in the following way. The first thing to keep in mind is that the study of *the relationship* between two entities is different from trying to understand *the entity itself.* The former is the basis for a holistic study while the latter is the method of reductionism. In a holistic approach the aim is to discover underlying themes in a phenomenon following certain procedures. This process results in a cognized whole, which may vary from a visual 'Gestalt' of a pattern to an all encompassing 'Gaia.' The

'Gestalt' is a unitary perception, an emergent property (Rock & Palmer, 1990). The 'Gaia' signifies a network of relationships among the elements or parts of a complex system, the Earth, which gives an impression of a single living entity (Lovelock, 1979). In both these cases one proceeds from above to below.

Natives, for example, perceive the frequent occurrence of landslides in the Himalayas due to something wrong in the relationships among the parts of the entire eco-system. They do not consider it an isolated event caused due to one or more factors related to geological structure of the mountain system. Modern scientists, however, defend the latter point of view. A native may proceed in his reasoning like this: people crave for more and more money from timber, denude trees on the hill slopes and side by side intensify agriculture. They perceive it as an interference in natural phenomena, consequently there is unpredictable weather, spells of dryness and cloudbursts, and the bare landscape starts eroding and slowly chunks of landmass slide down. The native thinks in terms of inter-relatedness among various parts of the ecosystem. These constituent parts of the ecosystem may be physical, social and psychological. Among the psychological constituents comes the pleasure and displeasure of local deities as well as universal gods and goddesses. In other words, the material and the spiritual integrate meaningfully in native's mind.

Long time ago, in a series of Gifford Lectures, Frazer (1926) explored the worship of nature in distant parts of the world including India. In his opinion the materialist and the spiritualist theories aim at knowing the ultimate reality, which '*is beyond the immediate data of sense*.' In recent times a psychoanalyst (Kakar, 2001) has explored the relationship between culture and healing in different parts of India. He observes that for masses the harmonious integration with one's group and surrender to the supreme power is perhaps natural and has healing properties. One must, however, be extremely careful about the procedures involved in the traditional healing practices. In the cognition of a native his deities interact at various levels ranging from his social milieu to his search for the ultimate reality of the cosmos.

In the collective consciousness of natives, the development is a quest for *atm-gyan* or self-enlightenment but at the same time one has to work for *sarvodaya* or welfare of all following the principle of *advaita* or non-dualism. There are several developmental interventions in the Garhwal Himalaya, which have been creating cognitive dissonance in the minds of native people. The cognitive dissonance occurs due to a mismatch between the native's and the government's versions of models of development in the hills. It has led to the two widely debated actions of the natives of Garhwal Himalaya: conflicts over the felling of green trees (Bahuguna, 1982; Mira Behn, 1978; Singh, 2001), and dissent over the construction of big dams (Bahuguna, 1978; Bhatt, 1992; Pirta, 2001; Valdiya, 1992).

Modern technocrats, however, disagree with the native's conceptualization of development. Therefore some criteria of development are needed. A psychologist, Tripathi (2002) proposes the criteria of openness and embeddedness for any change to be considered as development. If we follow these two criteria to test the validity of the large-scale interventions in the Himalayas as models of development, the result would probably be negative. First of all, even well known scientists have questioned the openness of large scale interventions in the Himalayas such as big dams (Valdiya, 1992). The other reason is more important and partly includes the first one in it. Many voluntary social workers who have devoted their lives for openness in the hill society, are disillusioned by the lack of embeddedness of the local people in these large projects (Bahuguna, 1978; Bhatt, 1992). This is probably the main cause of the native's struggle against the large-scale interventions in the Himalayas. No doubt these interventions create enormous social as well as physical change, they hardly meet the criteria of development, either for a native or for the psychologist.

In this section an attempt has been made to relate the concepts used by the native people with the concepts used by the social psychologists. There appears to be a considerable similarity both in the meaning of concepts and underlying processes. Some of those concepts and processes are harmony, holism, development and the relationship of thinking, feeling and behaving. The following section summarizes the research, which we have been conducting in the Himachal Pradesh University on the applications of the assumptions based on the native cognition of sustainable development presented above. These studies have social relevance and deal with issues of theoretical significance in environmental psychology. The problems that have been explored, broadly speaking, pertain to areas of: pro-environmental behaviour, emotional attachment systems, and humanist versus authoritarian approaches.

Application of the Natives' Cognitive Model

A major achievement of the Chipko Movement is its holistic approach that has made significant contribution in creating environmental consciousness among people. Its significance (Berreman, 1989) lies in '*the hope that Chipko holds for the people of the Himalayas, and as a model for the people of India.*' This native movement is an uprising against the materialistic values that regard nature as a commodity for the use of human beings. In this respect the Chipko Movement is nearer to the Deep Ecology. For deep ecologists (Rotnenberg, 1993) the goal is '*a sustainable world where humanity thinks more than its own welfare.*' In passing, it is to be noted that Arne Naess, the founder of deep ecology (Naess, 1989), and the pioneers of the Chipko Movement were followers of Gandhian approach.

In our first study, the aim was to evaluate the effectiveness of the approach of the Chipko Movement in creating environmental awareness. Three groups—a control, experimental-I and experimental-II, were compared for environmental concern before and after delivering instructions. Experimental group-I and II, both received similar information for five days on the Chipko Movement and its holistic approach. However, the experimental group-II received extra information of waste management on four additional days. The effect of information on the participants has been compared on three components of environmental concern—awareness, behaviour and intention (Goswami & Pirta, 2001, 02). The treatment groups differed from the control group significantly on the environmental concern (Figure 6.2). However, the additional information on waste management to experimental group-II had no effect. Thus the influence of holistic approach in creating environmental concern was quite evident in the study. At the same time, it would appear that the holistic approach of the Chipko Movement is more influential in creating environmental consciousness among people than the other behavioral approaches. This, however, needs further exploration.

In the second study, our objective was to find out whether the displacement has negative effects on the social and psychological well-being of oustees. Our assumption was that the displacement would impair the emotional attachment systems in individuals, families, and communities, which are essential for normal social behavior. This assumption has its basis in the attachment theory in psychology, which has much wider application in conjunction with the native cognitive model of development. On this basis we have been theorizing that the breakdown of emotional bonds due to displacement lead to an imbalance in the thinking, feeling and behavior of an individual.

Fig. 6.2: Holistic instructions improved environmental concern

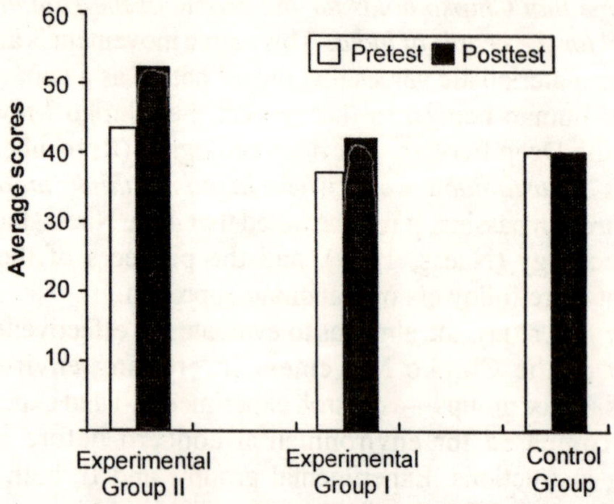

After conducting observations and interviews on the displacees of Tehri Dam in their alien habitats, our suggestion is that displacement should be avoided as far as possible because of its negative consequences and human apathy (Pirta, 2003; Pirta & Agrawal, 2003). Similar findings have reported for Pong Dam (Anonymous, 1991) and Bhakra Dam (Chandel & Pirta, 2003) oustees (Figure 6.3).

The rehabilitation process is so difficult that the problems of Bhakra Dam and Pong Dam oustees have not been solved even after about forty years. In this context we must realize that according to the World Health Report 2001 on mental health, there are more than 50 million people who have been displaced due to natural and man made disasters, and are mostly in the developing countries. Social psychiatrists observe that there is breakdown of community support system in such cases but it is also accompanied by the separation from loved objects. These two factors though separate from one another negatively affect the psychological aspects of the health of displacees. Our study suggests that it is advisable to move an entire village, keeping the social structure intact, to a site that is as physically proximate to the native area as far as possible. Oustees should receive counseling to cope up with the trauma of dislocation and to manage acculturative stress. The guidelines for this counseling process should come from a holistic approach, where one has respect for nature and recognizes the interdependence in its elements.

Fig. 6.3: Oustees of Bhakra Dam reported poor mental health

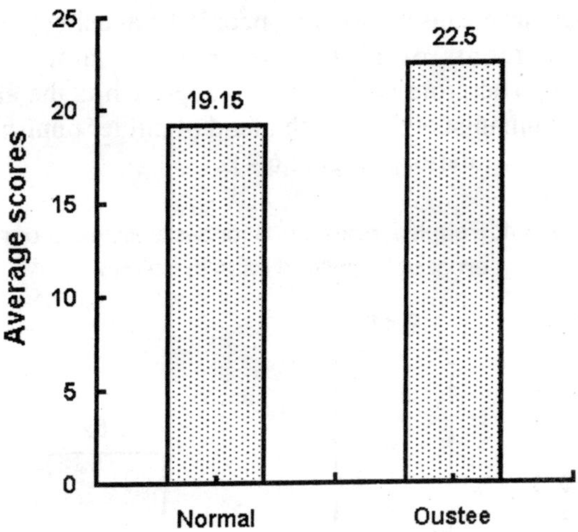

In the third study, our aim was to examine the implications of native's approach to understand the acute problem of the disposal of polyethylene bags in the cities. Some Indian states have decided to impose a ban on the use of polyethylene bags in public places. Their measures, however, are highly stringent, which include a severe penalty and imprisonment for carrying a polyethylene bag. This is an authoritarian approach to solve an environmental problem. In contrast an integrative approach may prove more effective to deal with the problem. The holistic model of Chipko emphasizes the *samagra* or integrative approach to such environmental issues, which require the participation of general public. It follows *manviya* or the humanist viewpoint where the equitability of participation, sustainability in resource use and democratic process in decision making guide the resolution of conflict on an issue.

Our survey of various socio-ecological habitats in the city of Shimla indicates that despite the ban, following an authoritarian approach, most of the people still carry polyethylene bags in public places (Sethi & Pirta, 2001). People of Shimla 'completely agreed' with the humanistic approach involving education, cooperation of the government and the public, direct public participation, public opinion and provision of alternatives to stop the people from using polyethylene bags. Considering authoritarian approach; involving fines, closing polyethylene manufacturing units, using strict rules and regulations, using all possible authoritative measures and imprisonment as means of stopping people from using polyethylene bags, the residents of Shimla are perhaps more or less in disagreement. Therefore an integrative approach is the alternative, which has a humanist outlook with blend of milder punishments but uses rules and regulations (Figure 6.4).

Fig. 6.4: Peoples' preference for two policies of ban on of polyethylene bags in Shimla

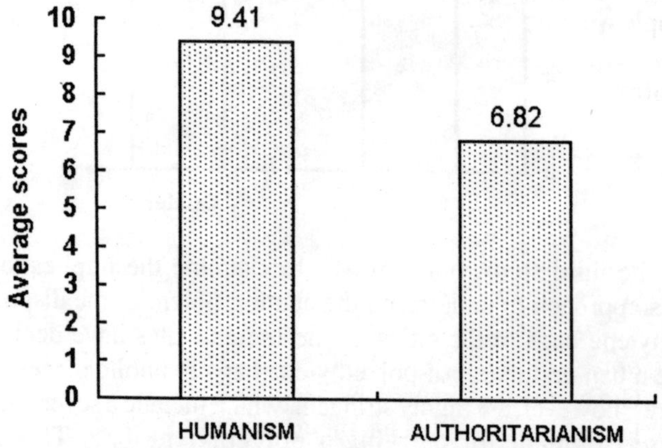

In summary, the natives' cognition has potential for application in environmental sciences. First, it may, for example, help us to understand a pro-environment action in the form of thinking, feeling and behaving. It appears that the holist approach of Chipko is influential in creating environmental consciousness among people. Second, it should be possible to examine the consequences of displacement and rehabilitation in terms of deviation from the native's cognitive model in conjunction with the attachment theory. Third, people tend to favour a humanist approach, a characteristic of holist view, rather than authoritarian policies to solve environmental problems.

Furthermore, knowledge seekers would find the interaction of people with their forest gods, water spirits, ghosts and demons full of curious phenomena. We can explore the institution of local deity in relation to the general well-being of people. In recent years a socio-ecologist, Crook (1997) has explored the indigenous psychiatry in some parts of Western Himalaya and found these culture specific mental phenomena, for example the possession by deities, interesting. On the contrary, it is difficult to understand the puritan attitude of social scientists towards these "little traditions" (worship of local deities), though they are interested in studies on the consciousness (Rao, 2001). The indifference of the academicians to such phenomena should not come in our way while we join a social scientist Kenneth Gergen[3] in the resistance against the Western colonization of mental health. The last chapter of this report explores this issue in the institution of deity for its role in the outer and inner environment of the people of Himachal Pradesh.

End notes

1. David Mitrany has discussed this conflict between the cognitive beliefs of two great leaders of India in the introduction to Pyarelal's book.
2. These naturalistic observations inspired Pirta to undertake studies on two common Indian monkeys that has relevance to this issue (Pirta, R.S. 1990. *Cooperation in urban macaques and langurs*. Department of Science and Technology, Government of India, New Delhi).
3. From the unpublished manuscript of Kenneth J. Gergen (Gergen, K.J. The self: Colonization in psychology and society. Downloaded on 3rd August 2005 from___*http://www.swarthmore.edu/SocSci/kgergen1*) and personal communication through email in August 2005.

7

Institution of Deity

An important question that has always bothered the people of India is to seek unity in diversity. But in his foreword to the introductory volume of the *People of India* (POI) series, an eminent social scientist, M.N. Srinivas (2002) writes, "*We should first of all ask for acceptance of diversity*." In this ancient and resilient culture, he believes, there is always an undercurrent of homogenization. It would be a fallacy to see integration only at the ideational or symbolic levels, cautions Singh (2002) in the same volume while summarizing the voluminous data of the POI project. For him, more important is the sharing of space, ethos, and traits. There is ample evidence in the POI data that the process is going on at the grassroots level. We have to act as catalysts in this interaction.

In the enormous POI survey, an interesting dimension of the sharing has emerged in the correlation of traits among various communities of India when grouped into socio-religious categories. For example, there is a very high correlation between the Hindu and Sikh, the Hindu and Muslim, the Hindu and Jain, and the Hindu and Buddhist. The data show that the traits related to religion, power, and dominance are more important than the other traits. There is participation in each other's religious ceremonies and festivals and the visiting of each other's shrines is also high.

From Myth to Reality

These observations based on the grassroots data from the whole of India suggest that at the local level, it would be worthwhile to look for micro-level analysis of the institutions where people associate with each other. The institution of deity in the state of Himachal Pradesh is the live example of such social-religious institutions where people come together to share various aspects of life at the local, regional, state and even at the national and international levels. For example, the festival of Kullu Dashehra is now celebrated as an international event.

The analysis of the POI project data by the Center for Ecological Sciences at the I.I.Sc., Bangalore (Joshi, Gadgil & Patil, 1993) has added a significant dimension to it. Some of the findings of these analyses have been discussed in Chapters 1 & 4, there is an important point that needs mention here. In comparison to the adjacent states (Table 7.1), the number of communities in Himachal Pradesh is higher. Even the number of the traits within a single community is the highest—406 for Khashia—in all over India. We can hypothesize that this rich cultural diversity is conducive for a congenial atmosphere within a state.

The state of Himachal Pradesh is predominantly rural and people are dependent on agriculture. The traditional culture is the dominant mode of life. When one looks at the local level, there is diversity of socio-religious institutions. Each village or complex villages have their own deity. The major events taking place in the life of the individual, the family and the village takes place through the institution of deity. These local deities are linked at the regional, state and at the national level.

Table 7.1: Comparison of Himachal Pradesh with other states on some parameters measured in the People of India (POI) Project (Joshi, Gadgil & Patil, 1993)

States	*No. of communities*	*Mean no. of traits*	*Mean dissimilarity*	*Total no. of traits*	*Population (millions)*		
					1981	1991	2001
Himachal Pradesh	116	229.2	.348	698	4.281	5.171	6.078
Jammu & Kashmir	111	201.1	.454	691	5.987	7.719	10.144
Punjab	95	192.2	.400	644	16.789	20.282	24.359
Uttar Pradesh	307	206.4	.413	721	110.862	139.112	174.687
Haryana	82	231.7	.336	636	12.923	16.464	21.145

For example, the local deity is taken on a pilgrimage to Yamunotri, Gangotri, Badrinath and Kedarnath. This further supports our hypothesis that the institution of deity may provide useful linkages to understand the nature of cohesiveness among the hill people of Himachal Pradesh.

There are some other aspects of the institution of deity in Himachal Pradesh that have significance with relation to human and nature relationship. For example, in context of indigenous technology the distinguished biologist, Verma (1998) has described two kinds of wood lots—the sacred wood lots and the private and community wood lots. The sacred wood lot is a practice to "*conserve and protect an entire forest or a small wood lot in the name of the village Deity (Kul Devata). This is prevalent in every village of the mountainous region of India, particularly so in Himachal Pradesh, Garhwal and Kumaon hills and also Kashmir hills. A temple along with a hut or shelter is constructed to keep the items/utensils of the village Diety. All religious rites are performed in its complex and no body is allowed to fell the trees. This is also a common practice in the hills of Kangra, Mandi and Shimla districts. It is also seen that a perennial water source is managed either in the forest or near it, for common use by the village for drinking purpose*." (Verma, 1998)

In an important study on the cultural and ecological dimensions of sacred groves in India. Malhotra, Chatterjee, Gokhale and Srivastava (2001) have mentioned that in Himachal Pradesh, the tradition of sacred groves is generally known as *dev van*. They report a relationship between the tradition of sacred groves and the dense forest cover in Shimla, Mandi, and Kullu districts. Moreover there were about 10,000 temples in the State with defined management committees and Biradari Panchayats (Caste councils). A majority of those deities were reported to have their own groves (Sharma, 2000).

While looking for a policy change in Himachal Pradesh, some investigators have reported the lack of conservation ethic among the people of Himachal Pradesh. This has been particularly voiced in the misuse of the Timber Distribution (TD) rights (Gouri, Mudgal, Morrison & Mayers, 2004). It is difficult to isolate the social processes behind this erosion and the intentions of the investigators. For example, they write that the timber mafia opposed the bill to modify the TD rights and the poor people "*wearing torn pyjamas and bussed into Shimla in a fleet of trucks*" to demonstrate loud and long — and the bill was shelved."

However they also think that the institution of deity can play an important role in forest preservation and community participation. They are of the opinion that "*At present, devta, gaon sudhar and mandir committees do not play any role in forest based livelihoods, but their membership is influential at the local level. There is potential for them to influence forest protection related decisions, promoting and facilitating the acceptance of various forest based livelihoods and also to support the marketing of produce. Devta committees are being registered under the Societies Act 1860 since 1997 and some of them are also getting transferred to the Kardaars (managers). There are cases where Kardaars have got the land transferred in their names, treating it as personal property.*" (Gouri, Mudgal, Morrison & Mayers, 2004)

Searching for the antecedents of a form of peasant resistance, the Dhoom, in Himachal Pradesh, Singh (2002) hypothesised community cooperation for survival in the hills. He argues that, "*Further reinforcing this environment-engendered co-operation was the emergence of a community 'consciousness'. This was also bolstered partly by a caste affinity and more so by a shared faith in a common folk devata. The hold that religious beliefs had upon the mind of the hill peasantry should not be underestimated. A combination of village-level co-operation (for economic reason) and community-consciousness (as socio-political phenomenon) was probably the organizing principle of rural life in the mountains. This interestingly, was also the factor that enabled the peasantry to resist unbridled exploitation by those in authority.*" (Singh, 2002) Although historical explorations, through the contemporary institutions of deities, are being pursued, an area of immense practical significance seems the mental health of people. The chapter focuses on this neglected aspect of the village *devata* where community evolves an institution for its holist development and particularly to meet the needs of higher order cognitive and mental functions.

Himachal Pradesh, is characterized with a unique integration of traditional and modern life patterns that appear complementary to each other. If some recent social and economic surveys are taken at its face value, Himachal Pradesh has emerged as a role model for the whole of the Himalayan region in terms of social harmony as well as progress. Although economists, in recent past, have attributed the progress of Himachal Pradesh to a strong tradition of local cooperative action, they did not elaborate upon the institutions that promote it. However, there is convincing evidence that the institution of deity provides the essential context for cooperative action and is closely associated with the mental health of people encompassing the physical, social and psychological aspects of their lives. The other most recent economic survey reiterates that Himachal Pradesh is the only state in India that combines a high level of social development with a high level of social equity. People perceive that besides the state administration, community participation is the key in the mountains of Himachal Pradesh for peaceful cohabitation and progress.

The evidence from these economic surveys affords sound basis for a community approach to the neglected area in the process of modern development, the mental health of people. This approach has significance due to lack of professionals in mental health care, remoteness of mountainous region, and weak financial resources. Therefore, it would be wise to make such a policy decision through which the institution of deity becomes the base for mental health care. The prevalence of institutions of deities and furthermore their resilience, diversity, and dynamism make them suitable spaces for promoting mental health services. Not only that, it may pave way for a new and healthy collaboration between traditional healers and professionals as envisaged by the World Health Organisation in 2001 for mental health in the developing countries. Moreover the Millennium Eco-system Assessment (MA) has recognized the overwhelming need to keep the well-being of human beings on the top of its agenda. The three aspects of well-being, the mental, the social and the physical are linked to the ecosystem services (Box 7.1).

Even the agnosticism towards spiritual and religious aspects has given way to a positive attitude towards such activities by considering them as the important component of the ecosystem services. In other words, besides the material services, the ecosystem services also include aesthetic enjoyment, recreation, artistic and spiritual fulfillment, and intellectual development. Earlier, from inorganic evolution there was a move toward organic evolution; the recent trend is in the direction of social-cultural-spiritual evolution. The recognition of the importance of the social, cultural and spiritual factors as important components of ecosystem services is likely to receive appreciation of the community of social scientists.

Box 7.1: The well-being of all

The *Millennium Ecosystem Assessment* (MA) accepts that the well-being of human beings is important and it is linked with the health of the eco-system. It is a phenomenal change. Since it has been expressed at global level through an endeavour of science, this is a unique event. Furthermore, the emphasis is to link the ecosystem services with quality of social institutions as well as the quality of interventions taking place within them.

The realization among material scientists about human well-being has resulted in a uniquely important change in their attitudes toward material and non-material. Unless this change in the attitude occurs globally among the human beings, the ecosystem would continue to change in an unpredictable manner and threaten the life support system. In this situation there may be few beneficiaries of the ecosystem services while a large segment of the human population may be the looser. The thrust of MA is on equitable use of ecosystem services. If this effort for equitable use of ecosystem services takes concrete shape in our policy and planning as envisaged by the scientists of MA, there is hope for a more civilized society.

The Millennium Ecosystem Assessment is spreading a new vision globally where the social and behavioural actions receive greater significance in the improvement of ecosystem and human well-being.

Peace and Cohesion

The deities and their abodes are part of the Indian culture. Historians record the prevalence of the deities all over India since ancient times; the urban areas and the trade routes supporting some of the largest temples whereas villages own smaller deities (Thapar, 2002). For some ecologists, these local deities and their folklore symbolize the conflicts of interests involving individuals and groups. This idea finds reflection in some fascinating research on *deoban* or sacred groves from various parts of India (Gadgil, 2001). The archetypes of institutions of deities have immense appeal for psychoanalysts. Finally, it remains for the humanist psychologists to explore the premises of the temple for the origin and development of a unique relationship between the deity and his devotee.

This relationship seems vital for mental health and assumes the properties of the therapist (deity) and the client (devotee). The mountains and people of the Himalayas forming the tiny state of Himachal Pradesh embody this unique divine relationship. The state is an integration of traditional and modern life patterns that appear complementary to each other. If some recent social and economic surveys have some face value, Himachal Pradesh qualifies as an appropriate role model for the whole of the Himalayan region in terms of social harmony as well as progress.

In the 1980s, one wondered about the peace that prevailed in Himachal Pradesh, when its surrounding states were in turbulence. For some cynics the calmness in Himachal Pradesh indicated apathy of people towards the modern developmental process. The theory found support in the unquestioning belief of these mountain people in local deities, suggesting a deep-rooted escapism or fatalism. But it was not true. While these mountain people felt proud of the deities, they were silently making a socio-economic revolution. They assimilated new knowledge with the traditional wisdom and acquired whatever was essential for survival in the harsh terrain. A conspicuous example is the transformation in traditional agriculture through cultivation of apple. There was no revolt against the tradition. The hill people modified it where necessary according to their needs.

Perhaps as a result of this process, at the dawn of twenty-first century, Himachal Pradesh registered a spectacular leap on various parameters of development. It was not very surprising, in view of the peace prevailing in this Himalayan state. Some economists attribute the progress to the local tradition of cooperative action, however they are unable to specify the institutions that promote this kind of pro-social behaviour (Dreze & Sen, 2002). But it seems that the institution of deity provides the essential context for cooperative action in a hill society. In addition, the institution of deity encompasses the physical, social, psychological and spiritual aspects of people's lives and may be regulating their mental well-being. It is reflected in the most recent economic survey in India in which Himachal Pradesh stands out as the only state in India where high level of social development associates with a high level of social equity (Saran, 2004). For an eminent leader of Himachal Pradesh, Virbhadra Singh, not only the state administration but the community participation also holds the key in the mountains of Himachal Pradesh for peaceful cohabitation and progress. Incidentally, he is also the custodian of the institution of goddess Bhima Kali, the principle deity of the erstwhile state of Bushahr.

There are other social and economic institutions also which relate people to each other. Some of them regulate sets of person's functionings associated with birth, death, marriage, kinship and livelihood. But these institutions in general subserve the institution of deity. For instance, in the Kiari area of Himachal Pradesh, the most progressive *panchayat* or the village council, in the whole of Asia, all villagers obey their deity, *Deo Boindra*. In one case, it was observed that a father took his son who had tumor in his brain to New Delhi, got him operated, but his survival seemed bleak. They finally left it to their local deity, *Deo Boindra*, who consoled them, but still the son died. So apparently the deity's worship was futile. But the father perhaps gained strength to face the inevitable, the death of his young son. There is an instance of a different nature from the same area. People were not observing social norms while making some new constructions around their houses. Many families had added new portions to their houses, which partly encroached upon the common pathway in the village. They cleared the new portions of their buildings, when asked by the deity, *Deo Boindra*, to do so. Those who saw it happen voluntarily, felt that it would have not been possible even by imposing a severe penalty. All that took place when the deity was on the move in its territory along with the community people. Most of the deities in the hills are moving gods. People carry them in palanquins from place to place within their territories for worship.

Deities may originate in modern times, too. First there is genesis of new myth within a kin group, and the hero becomes alive as a new deity. The group then begins the worship of the deity. For example, the devotees of the deity in the village Jhaladi as a part of the local population. Only one kin group worshipped the *Jhaladi ra Deo*, having a history of its origin, which was about 25-30 years old. Although the households in Jhaladi and its adjacent village Jatadi increased significantly in past few years, due to migration from nearby villages. They have not yet accepted the new deity, and still worship their ancestral deity.

The Social Institution

In order to find out the contribution of the institution of deity in the physical, social and mental life of the mountain people, we have been exploring the Shimla region of Himachal Pradesh. Our aim here is to illustrate the role of the institution of a deity *Shadi ra Deo* from the prosperous Jubbal valley of Shimla district in Himachal Pradesh in the cohesiveness among the members of the local community. In the Jubbal valley, part of a former hill state, people worship several local and Brahmanical (universal) deities, however the principal deity is *Shadi ra Deo*. It earlier had a status equivalent to the ruler of the Jubbal State (the *Raja*). Although there was change in the political institution of the *Raja,* after the independence of India in 1947, the institution of the *Shadi ra Deo* was not affected. In the latter case, the reasons for its survival may be the dynamic nature of the deity-follower relationship and the choice it entails to its follower for the other options in life. Thus on one hand the institution of deity provides a safe haven for a person where he finds relief from stresses and strains of life, and on the other hand it is a secure base from where one has enormous choice to explore the world.

For this it is essential to understand the functional social unit in a village and its relationship with the institution of deity. The *ghar* or household is an important social unit in a *gaon* or village. A *gaon* may consist of a number of *ghar*. Each *ghar* has one or more members who represent one or more generations, whose survival is largely dependent upon the land owned by each *ghar*. In each *gaon* several castes live together performing various roles complementary to each other and essential for the survival of the *gaon*. For example, the members of a caste specialising as musicians or *toories* (also known as *dhakies*) would cater to the needs of several *gaon* in the area.

Take for example the village Dakaod of the Jubbal valley. The total number of *ghar* in this village have increased from 16 in 1955-56 to 39 in 2002-03. They belong to two kin groups of the *khashia* (rajput) and the *bhat* (brahmin) castes (Table 7.2). Services of other castes needed by the villagers of Dakaod are met from adjacent villages. Their livelihood is agriculture but besides that each *ghar* has at least one member in a government job. About half of the families from both the castes have migrated to their ancestral land at higher altitude, used earlier as summer pasture for cattle, sheep and goat. But in these pastures villagers now grow potatoes and apples. These two crops are responsible for an economic revolution in the region.

Table 7.2: Showing the socio-economic features of the deity in the village of Dakaod

S. No.	*Year of Worship (Bharanshi)*	*Economic Activity (Rupees)*			*Families (Ghar)*	
		Income	*Expenditure*	*Saving*	*Bhat (Brahmin)*	*Khashia (Rajput)*
1.	1955–56	158	147	11	7	9
2.	1960–61	515	204	311	7	9
3.	1966–67	517	169	348	9	12
4.	1971–72	1353	1337	16	11	13
5.	1987–88	9742	4645	5097	10	18

Each *ghar* in the village of Dakaod obeys the *kara* of *Shadi ra Deo*, the rules and regulations of the deity (Table 7.3). The *kara* is an unwritten Constituion, which is assimilated by the individual as he grows up in the *gaon*. The institution of deity receives various forms of support from the devotees.

Table 7.3: The villages that abide by the *kara* of the *Shadi ra Deo*

Bharanshi worshippers	*Bharanshi non-worshippers*
1. Shadi 2. Chamaru 3. Dakaod 4. Purana Jubbal 5. Kiyari	6. Jatadi 7. Jhaladi 8. Naktada 9. Salaokra 10. Choontada 11. Rampuri 12. Dharai 13. Deem 14. Gadnu 15. Khada Pathar 16. Odi 17. Madan 18. Navari 19. Mandhaik 20. Jachali
These five villages worship the deity for one year each in the above order. This is termed as the *bharanshi*. After one year the deity moves to the next village. The deity is believed to have its origin in the village of Shadi. Therefore the *bharanshi* starts from Shadi village. The remaining villages observe all the rules and regulations and contribute voluntarily to the deity at the time of festivals.	21. Paraonthi 22. Bhagoli 23. Balroli 24. Kolada 25. Sirthi 26. Sundali 27. Nainar 28. Labdot 29. Pouta 30. Devara (a small town named Jubbal)

Each *ghar* contributes voluntarily in the form of manual service, agricultural produce (*jhakhadi*) and monetarily (*phant*). The contributions also come as offerings (*bhaint*) in the form of gold, silver, articles and cash. The manual service is needed in various forms and differs according to occasions. When there is a festival in the village, such as *jagara*, every individual of the *gaon* participates. However, the movement of the deity in space requires services of one male member from each family—the upper caste people (*bhat* and *khashia*) carry the palanquin of deity and other decorations, the musicians (*toori*) play musical instruments, and others (*koli*) carry the beating drums or *nagadas*.

There are temples (*deothi*) for *Shadi ra Deo* in the five villages and they worship the deity in turn, which comes every fifth year, starting from the *Shadi* village. The year of worship in each village is known as *bharanshi*. The *bharanshi poojan*, the worship of *Shadi ra Deo* is a collective decision of the *gaon* (Table 7.4).

Table 7.4: Comparison of duties, and contribution by the families during the two periods of *bharanshi poojan*

Major decisions	*Bharanshi 1955-1956 (Sept. 1955 to 12-9-1956)*	*Bharanshi 2002-2003 (13-9-2002 to 2-9-2003)*
Total *ghar* or families involved	There were 16 ghar or families. (whole *gaon* or village)	There were 39 ghar or families. (whole *gaon* or village)
Appointment of the *pujari* or priest for morning and evening *poojan* or worship of the deity in the temple for one year and their *hak* or remunerations	Pujara Moutu of Shadi	Pandit Laik Ram of Rampuri
	Two time meals or *theela* in turn by each family.	To be paid Rupees 12,000/- for *bharanshi poojan* (Rs.350/- per family)
	Each house provided *jhakhadi* of four *patha* each during the two crop seasons, *Kattik* and *Asad*. In the month of *Magh*, each family has to pay one rupee each to the priest of the deity.	Rs. 200/- per family for jhakhadi and for *theela*.

(*Contd.*)

(*Contd.*)

Major decisions	*Bharanshi 1955-1956 (Sept. 1955 to 12-9-1956)*	*Bharanshi 2002-2003 (13-9-2002 to 2-9-2003)*
Appointment of *toori* or musician for beating drums during morning and evening *pooja* and the *nabad* at night.	Toori Nika Ram Two times meals or *theela* in turn by each family. Each house provided *jhakhadi* of four *patha* each during the two crop seasons, *Kattik* and *Asad.*	Indaru Toori To be paid Rs. 8,000/- per year (Rs. 215 per family) and two times meals or *theela* family in turn by each family (or Rs. 300 per year).
The duty of *chauki* (night watch) of the deity, one adult male from each *ghar* has to sleep at night in the temple of the deity.	Three to four members (one from each family) each night, throughout the year. Four *ghar* were relieved from the duty of *chauki* due to elder member's job or old age or illness or old age.	Three to four members (one from each family) each night, throughout the year. Now half of the villagers were living away from the village and did not participate in *chauki*, they compensated it in other ways.
Tambi (measure of ghee for *poojan* and *dhoop*). One and half tambi is to be used for poojan during each month; and one tambi each for the festivals of *Badi Saji*, *Maghi*, *Baisakhi*, *Savan*, *Jatar* and *Jagara*.	Each family contributed one *Tambi* of *ghee* during the year.	A contribution of Rs.100/- per family for the *poojan* (same as in 1955-56; but the ghee is purchased from the market).

Source: Documents by Rama Saran Pirta and B.S. Pirta.

Each *ghar* is involved in this decision and invites the deity from the preceding village on the occasion of the *Jagara* festival. All the five *bharanshi* worshipping villages and people from other villages participate in the *Jagara poojan* (also known as *panjvi ki raat* or fifth day after the *Amavasya* or new moon that generally falls in the month of September). This is the last day of *bharanshi poojan* in the particular village, and next day the deity remains as a guest of the village. Few members (the *kardars* or functionaries of the deity) from the next village, which is due for *bharanshi*, comes in the morning and extends an invitation to the deity on behalf of their village.

This takes place early in the morning when the *Jagara* function has ended and the deity possesses the *mali*. The deity thanks the villagers who worshipped the *bharanshi*, blesses them and also resolves some personal or social conflicts brought to his notice. The members of the prospective village, who have come to invite the deity, give assurance that they are happy to invite the deity and would abide by the *kara*. The deity gives his consent, and the next day the whole village, one male member from each family, come to take *Shadi ra Deo* to their village. While the deity is decorated for movement to the other village, all the items that are part of the deity's procession are documented in the presence of members from both the villages. And each village keeps the copy of the movable items of the deity. The procession starts in the afternoon and reaches the destined village by evening.

Mental Health for All

The following sections describe some important mental concepts prevailing in the institution of *Shadi ra Deo*. The institution has similarity with other institutions of deities in the Western Himalayas and thus some general understanding of the healing system customary in these mountains is possible. The typical system in the institution of deity for healing mental problems involves the deity, the abode of the deity, the functionaries of deity, the villages worshipping the deity (the territory), and the natural milieu. But the most distinctive characteristic of the institution is the assumed presence of the divine in the temple, the dual nature of the deity. Thus the material and the non-material elements constitute the system, which include the deity and its functional aspects. Furthermore, every household interacts with these elements in terrestrial and non-terrestrial ways.

One learns these ways of behaving, thinking and feeling while growing up as a member of the institution of deity. This process may start even before the birth, during the intrauterine life of the child, a wish of parents for a child that may have been fulfilled by the deity. After the birth, it is customary to visit the deity and thus the child is introduced to the deity even when his declarative memory is undeveloped. Thus the early interactions of the person and his deity are part of the procedural memory. In other words, these memories develop when the person is not conscious about the events occurring around him.

These learning experiences, though taking place when the child's cognitive abilities are not well developed, occur in an atmosphere charged with emotion. There is a longing for the security of the child by the parents from the deity, which is expressed in a socially sanctioned way. Therefore these events may also form part of emotional memories. As the child grows up he also seeks the blessings of the deity by priming from the mother and other family members. Later it may occur through imitation and social facilitation. But at the same time his kin and age-mates caution him about the rules and regulations of the institution. Slowly the child acquires knowledge about the sacred space, social structure around the deity and the divineness (*saot*) of the deity.

In this way, through observational learning, occasional reinforcing and witnessing the consequences of polluting the sacred, the child implicitly and explicitly develops his 'schemata' of the institution of the deity in his mind. The ecological, social and mental aspects of the institution of deity get enriched with the individual's development in the cultural milieu. And at a certain stage the deity's figure manifests in his 'imagery' as protector, saviour, helper and companion. Thus the deity becomes maternal and paternal caregiver and sometimes this identification is gender specific as there are *devis* (female deities) and *devatas* (male deities). There is generalization from human (parental) caregiver to divine caregiver that involves learning and memory principles. Ultimately the institution of deity becomes a safe haven and secure base for the person.

Furthermore, the greater internalisation of the roles of the institution makes some person not only more attached to the deity but he becomes deity's functionary (*kardar* or *thani*). In some extreme cases an individual becomes the *mali* (spokesperson) of the deity. People believe that when the *mali* goes into trance (*tyari* or *otarna*), he speaks on behalf of the deity.

Some kind of social learning and training makes the *mali* of the deity perform this task, a kind of traditional healing through possession, according to the norms of the deity's institution. In the beginning the person gets possessed by the deity (*tyari*) during the festivals when the whole environment is under intense devotional emotion. He feels very high affective arousal and performs seemingly irrelevant motor activities and his verbalizations are sometimes incomprehensible. The contents of these verbalizations are emotionally charged and appear procedural in nature. But later on, the person undergoes possession by the deity only during social and therapeutic rituals to sort out specific problems. Due to these experiences of possession the person becomes a socially accepted *mali* (spokesperson) of the deity. Now the *mali's* behaviour appears under his control and there is coherence in his replies.

A common observation is that the *mali* seldom remembers what he speaks and performs in the state of trance. It further suggests the role of procedural (emotional type) memories during the state of possession. However, some observations of the therapy by possession suggest two very significant elements in it, consciousness and prediction. There is some content of consciousness in the *mali's* words. And thus it also involves declarative memory. Though the decisions of the *mali* suggest some higher states of consciousness, one may not be sure about its prophetic nature. The devotees obey them willingly as deity's word. But at the same time it is also true that the devotees have freedom to find out alternative solutions.

The devotees, who at times are clients in need of therapy, also believe that not to follow the *kara*, the norms of the deity, is to annoy him, which means inviting trouble (*dosh*) for the household. These cognitions receive ample reinforcement from the oral and written systems of the religion. For example, the numerous stories in the holy books, the life histories of saints, and the personal experiences narrated by people, all these sources provide rich material for the development of cognitive schemas where an array of positive and negative expectancies form intricate patterns of attachment with the deity and the other spirits. Where the overall positive and negative expectations of the person from the deity interact with person's perception of own actions as positive and negative. Thus there may be four broad matrices of the deity-devotee interaction, namely secure, insecure, ritualistic and fearful.

The healing by the deity's *mali* has some similarities with the behaviour therapy approach in psychology. The behaviour therapist does not spend his time and effort to ascertain causes but his primary focus is the present disorder of the client and its modification by following the principles of learning. Although the *mali* and the behaviour therapist may suggest some cause of the problem, they do not insist on it, the whole emphasis is on learning new relationships with the physical, social and psychological environment. Invariably there is suggestion of some correctional measure, which involves manipulation of environmental events in such a way that they act as positive and negative reinforcers. In addition, the verbal reinforcement of the deity's *mali* and the behaviour therapist is extremely important. Apparently, the *mali* has more control on the environmental contingencies than the therapist. It is because the *mali* can elicit support from the deity's well-knit institution. Though behaviour therapist has no inclination towards the divine factors, sometimes he may consider the cultural factors.

In both kinds of therapies the cause and cure are external to the subject. Moreover, the whole effort is on reconciliation between the two parties. But they have choice. Thus the probability of a response in both kinds of therapies is almost similar. The response may increase or decrease according to the nature of reinforcement (positive or negative) and its delivery or withdrawal. But the success of the behaviour therapist, as well as the *mali* of the deity, depends on how far they are able to manipulate the contingencies of the environmental stimuli. The extent to which they are able to manipulate (deliver or withdraw) the reinforcement to the client is largely dependent upon the nature of the institution.

It is significant to note that the *mali's* effort strengthens the institution of deity, materially as well as non-materially. His personal gain is almost negligible. The client offers some *bhaint* or present to the deity after fulfillment of the *ichha* or will that may be of considerable value. It may be a penalty or *dand* and the contribution may also come from *bondh* (offer), *pooja* (worship) and *bali* (sacrifice) where the aim is to appease the deity. Most of the donations come from normal individuals. All this goes to the institution of deity. Furthermore, the efficiency of the *mali* strengthens belief in deity. The possession of the *mali* plays the central role in the healing process of vast variety of cases brought to the institution of the deity.

If some person or party accepts the deity's decision, he would be free from the assumed annoyance or *dosh* of the deity. But he may have to do something for the appeasement of the deity, and on some occasions to satisfy the demands of other good or bad spirits. In case the other party is not ready to abide by the deity's decision, a unilateral sanction is enforced, and the other party or individual may then be liable for further annoyance of the deity. In some rare cases, the deity suggests *chhuan* or severing of all physical and social relations with the disobeying party, which may be a close kin. It shows that people uphold the sanctions of the institution of deity in great esteem and abide by it. Land disputes are a common cause of differences among people in rural areas. Here is a case that explains the concept of *chhuan* between the two families in the village of Darkoti who were kin.

The *chhuan* lasted for over fifty years during which the lone lady, the victim, and the individuals of the rival family, who were primarily involved in the dispute had passed away. But the *chhuan* continued to be practiced by their descendents. Though the relations between the two families had improved a lot, they continued to practice the *chhuan* in fear of the deity's annoyance. Finally, in 2003 the two families agreed upon ending the *chhuan*. For this they approached the *deity*, the *Mahasu* and both the parties expressed their mutual desire to end the *chhuan*. The *mali* of the *Mahasu*, under the possession of the deity, recommended the following procedure to do away with the *chhuan* between the two families. Both the parties gave a *Jagara* of the *Mahasu* in their village, which involved the night worship of the deity in which the whole village participated and the expenditure was borne by the affected parties. Next, the male members of both the families accompanied by some villagers visited the birthplace of *Mahasu* at Hanol, far away from their village. Here they offered a *bali* or sacrifice of a ram or *khadu* to *Mahasu* and asked for his blessings. This is how the *chhuan* that had existed for over five decades ended and both the families once again resumed cordial relations.

The institution of deity has physical, social and psychological functions essential for the survival of *ghar* or household and its inmates who are close kin. The activities occurring inside the *ghar* have close linkages with higher-level institutions; the *gaon* is the next in the hierarchy. However, the center and the state also mediate in the functioning of the *gaon* through political, social and developmental processes and through *panchayat*, a council of villages. Despite the fact that the *panchayat* is ideally the basic unit of the Indian democracy, for the last fifty years, its role in the area of mental health is non-existent. In comparison to it the institution of deity, which includes a village or a complex of villages, is particularly involved in the mental well-being of people from ancient to modern times. Some international organisations such as the World Health Organisation (WHO) are also working in various health programmes. It is true that the indigenous institutions as well as the national and international organizations are important in the area of health. But the people in the remote Himalayas have easy access to their deities, especially for mental health.

Need for Development of the Institution

The brief scenario of the institution of deity, presented above, provides an optimistic image of the future of this institution. However, it seems now that the institution is struggling for its survival. The following section narrates some issues related to the institution of deity which mirrors the widening gap between 'tradition' and 'science.'

In order to overcome these problems, and to increase the contribution of this traditional institution in the area of mental health, there is need to arrive at a considerate opinion on the pragmatic and socio-psychological aspects of the institution of deity.

Pragmatic Aspects

The *bharanshi poojan* involves great responsibility on the part of the villagers. Each *ghar* participates in it. All decisions are taken collectively. The process starts a few days before *bharanshi poojan*, when the villagers take several important decisions. Over the years it is becoming difficult to appoint a *pujari* or priest and a *toorie* or a musician. Their services are required in the morning and in the evening without failure, over one year. Since the traditional caste system and the performance of specific roles in the society is vanishing, it is becoming difficult to hire these persons, whether it be the priest or the musician.

This is one of the reasons for changes in the institution of deity. Those changes might be related to making the role of some persons, such as *pujari* and *toorie*, much wider and separate from their traditional caste based roles.

For this change, there is need for greater investment by the village community for widening the roles to be performed and loosening the caste system where there is an element of social discrimination. Besides the financial requirements needed for the worship of the deity that people are ready to meet, the problem may arise in the form of personal presence required for various tasks and its gender specific nature. For example, the *chauki* system (or night watch) requires that during the entire period of *bharanshi*, for one year three to four male members (one from each *ghar*) sleep each night in the *deothi*, the temple of the deity. Some male members however are not able to attend to this task due to being in service away from the village.

These problems may be resolved if some individuals are permanently employed, they can perform multiple roles and stay in the temple premises, as was the tradition. Since the cost of living has increased, it is becoming difficult for some persons to perform caste specific roles, irrespective of whether one is from the upper caste (the priest or *pujari*) or from the lower caste (the musician or *toorie*). Thus diversification and intensification of roles beyond the worship of the deity is needed. While we need such change in the institution of deity, our objectives should be in consonance with the main function of the institution of deity. The only area where the traditional goals of the institution of deity and the psychological need of the modern society meet each other is the mental health of people.

Various other activities needed at the village level may be in the areas of environment, education, health and employment. For example, the priest of the deity at Dakaod during 2003-04 was worshipping three deities in a day and also looked after the accounts of a cooperative society. Thus it is possible that with some additional training and education, the priest may function as a teacher or a health worker in the village. Not only that, sometimes the priest is also the *mali* (spokesperson) of the deity. Therefore in his alternative role, the priest can assist a clinical psychologist as a social-psychiatric caseworker. Whereas in the past, there was not much transaction of money in cash, but now the finances are regularly maintained in the institutions of deities and they also have bank accounts. In the larger institutions of deities even the government is appointing an administrator and other staff, besides the temple management committee, to look after the accounts and various functions of the temple. As far as participation in other activities is concerned, some of the institutions of deities already have orchards, schools, colleges and a number of other resources.

Here we provide some comparative information from an institution, The Divine Life Society (DLS), which was established near Rishikesh in the Himalayan foot-hills by a saint, Swami Sivananda in 1936. Although the major objective of the DLS was spiritual; uplifting of people following the Vedanta philosophy, it soon became involved in various activities needed in the region. The major source of income continues to be the donation from people, which shows tremendous increase over the years (Table 7.5). While the main purpose of DLS is the search for ultimate truth and purification of mind or mental hygiene (Chidananda, 1991; Sivananda, 1994), it is also doing pioneer work in the eradication of caste based discrimination and improving the lot of lepers. The moral, social and monetary support to environmental activities and movements in the Garhwal Himalaya by the DLS is also significant. The society also runs physical health centers and an academy for yoga. A large number of elderly people are spending a fruitful life at the DLS headquarters and its branches. The life of these elderly people at DLS is entirely different from the isolated life of elderly people living in old age care homes.

Table 7.5: Main heads of income and expenditure of The Divine Life Society, Shivanandanangar, Uttaranchal

	YEARS				
	1995-96	*1996-97*	*1997-98*	*1998-99*	*2002-03*
INCOME					
From donations	138*	143	157	177	251
EXPENDITURE**					
Hospital	22	31	35	40	68
Dissemination of knowledge	15	16	17	19	20
Social welfare	05	23	18	10	05
Leprosy relief	10	08	08	13	22
Annakshetra	31	34	37	40	48
Mandir	10	12	12	14	19
Ashram expenses	34	34	38	38	54

* All figures are in lacs, if the remaining amount in any entry was above 75,000, one was added to the total of that cell. These data are based on the Annual Report and Accounts of the respective years.

** There are number of other important activities in which the money is being spent such as natural calamities, agriculture farm, *goshala* (cowshed), cultural and spiritual tours, etc.

In this way we find that these institutions are already serving an important role that is somewhat parallel to the mental health in the sphere of psychology. There are, however, some significant differences between the two. There is a major difference in the classification of mental disorders, diagnostic methods and therapeutic procedures. We find such differences between psychiatry and clinical psychology on one hand, and within the various schools of psychology on the other. Incidentally, some schools of psychotherapy, primal therapy, transpersonal therapy and psychosynthesis, have some elements common with the traditional healing practices used in the institution of deity. At the same time it is difficult to deny the fact that psychoanalysis has been interpreting traditional healing practices and various other socio-religious phenomena since its inception (see Kakar, 2001 for Indian landscape in general; and see Ranchan, 2001; Ranchan & Justa, 1981 for regional interpretations). Although humanistic psychotherapy may have a lot in common with the institution of deity in theory, in practice the similarity of behaviour therapy (Bandura, 2001) with the healing method used in the institution of deity cannot be denied.

Socio-psychological Aspects

The traditional institution of deity is now becoming a mismatch with the processes of science and technology guiding modern development. We find that the socio-psychological function of the deity's institution is still prevalent but it is undermined by the materialistic paradigm. However, the major threat for the socio-psychological role of the institution of deity is from the social sciences itself as they aspire for material basis of their subject matter. Not denying the fact that materialist's discrimination stands against the social sciences as well. The social sciences are in dilemma to transcend from terrestrial to non-terrestrial realm. On the other hand, the natives, who worships the deity, has no difficulty in transcending between these two realms.

Sometimes psychologists also make transitions from biological (material) to mental (non-material). For example, consider the transition of Freud from physicalist to mentalist while developing the architecture of mind. His concepts still form the core of psychology. Behaviourist paradigm has also drifted from its physiological basis to the cognitive basis. Though they vehemently attack ethologists who are exploring the evolutionary basis of behaviour and refining methods of naturalistic observation.

Thus there are valid reasons to consider alternative hypotheses about mental issues. It is not uncommon to see that the native's causal analysis encompassing much wider range than the social scientist. The latter adhere to a particular school of thought. The native's mind transcends slowly from material to the non-material in his day to day life. Wherever possible, a native explains phenomena on the basis of material causation. For example, villagers are conscious of the material aspects of their deity, which is assumed as a divine source. When they see that the external decorations (*shringar*) of deity have worn out, donations are collected from public besides the obligatory contribution of the five villages to renew it. For example, the remoulding of the *shringar* items took about two months (Table 7.6). On the other hand, when causation is not possible in material terms, the native feels no difficulty in assuming some non-terrestrial causal factors.

Table 7.6: The remoulding of the *shringar* (ornamentation) of *Shadi ra Deo* in the year 2001*

Income		*Expenditure*	
Source	*Amount (Rupees)*	*Items*	*Amount (Rupees)*
Bharanshi worshipping villages Contributions (*Phant*)		Moulding cost	47,068
1. Shadi	8,000		
2. Chamaru	8,000		
3. Dakaod	8,000		
4. Purana Jubbal	8,000		
5. Kiyari	8,000		
Donations by others Note: It also included individual donations from the above villagers. Some help came in the form of silver and ration for the *bhandara* or community lunch.	15,034		
Offerings by devotees (*Bhaint*) (offerings of the day of *shuddhi* or purification ceremony)	12,999	Purification ceremony (*Shuddi*) and community lunch (*Bhandara*)	17,265
Grand Total (The balance was deposited in the account of the deity)	68,033		64,333

* A committee headed by the Sri Yogendra Chandra, the descendent of the Raja of Jubbal, having representatives from the villages looked after the whole affair.

It is also true that the dominant western development paradigm has influenced the peasants of Himalayan region. Consequently, the people perceive the institution of deity as hindrance since it creates severe conflict in a person's day to day life. The native sometimes faces the problem of 'defending the institution of deity' rather than drawing strength from the deity for himself. Thus there are two different aspects of the problem when we look for some kind of modification in the institution of deity. The first argument is for creating change to strengthen the institution of deity from the onslaught of alien institutions. We suggest that this should be taken up at the level of developing the institution as a source of knowledge. Traditionally many of these institutions were places where people came to acquire knowledge, but now this function has become obsolete to a large extent.

The second argument is for creating change is to enhance the socio-psychological role of the institution in the area of mental health. Though the deity's institution is performing this role but in the traditional way. We do not have any modern institution of mental health, worth its name, in the vast rural sector. Mental health is low priority area for the policy makers (WHO, 2001) as well as psychologists (Pandey, 2004). Only the institutions of deities provide little hope for individuals or groups. They are the sites of refuge for helpless and hopeless people whatsoever might be the nature of the institutions and the rituals associated with them. For example, the deity, *Shadi ra Deo* went on a pilgrimage to four religious places in the Himalaya (*Char Dham Yatra*) after about twenty years in 1994 (Table 7.7). People were happy to participate in the pilgrimage but it involved a lot of walking, eating one meal per day, and spending long time away from home. It is difficult to follow these observances in the present times. Now there is need to make some modifications. Although people are ready to donate money, they find it difficult to exert physically for several days at a stretch. We do not conceive any deviation in the institution of deity from its assumed divine nature, but the aim is to augment it with complementary techniques from psychology and psychiatry.

In this section some points are highlighted, where on one hand, natives are seen supporting the institution of the deity by participating in it, but on the other hand, it is becoming difficult for them to continue some of the rituals associated with this institution. It is in this regard the pragmatic aspects and socio-psychological aspects of the institution of the deity needs development in a direction that is relevant in modern times. This would be possible once we generate a considerate opinion for strengthening these institutions as centers of community care.

Table 7.7: Pilgrimage to Yamunotri, Gangotri, Badrinath and Kedarnath by *Shadi ra Deo* from April 3, 1994 to May 30, 1994

INCOME		*EXPENDITURE*	
Source	*Amount (Rupees)*	*Items*	*Amount (Rupees)*
Bharanshi worshiping villages (contribution or *phant*)		Boarding and lodging of following pilgrims *Shadi ra Deo*	29,857
1. Shadi	6,950	1. Madan Singh, Shadi (Bhandari)	
2. Chamaru	8,000	2. Mahinder Singh, Shadi	
3. Dakaod	8,000	3. Dalip Singh, Shadi	
4. Purana Jubbal	8,000	4. Padam Singh, Shadi	
5. Kiyari	8,000	5. Amar Singh Chauhan, Chamaru	
*Villagers of Jhaladi (*Phant*)* (The *Jhaladi ra Deo* also accompanied the *Shadi ra Deo*, who bore its expenses)	2,687	6. Mohar Singh, Chamaru (Mali)	
		7. Hira Nand Sharma, Dakaod (Pujari)	
		8. Jodh Ram Sharma, Dakaod	
		9. Salig Ram Sharma, Dakaod	
		10. Chaman Singh, Dakaod	
Offerings by devotees (*bhaint*)	1,170	11. Narayan Dutt, Purana Jubbal (Pujari)	
		12. Jiya Lal Lolta, Purana Jubbal (Kardar)	
		13. Shamsher Singh Lolta, Purana Jubbal	
		14. Virender Singh Aukta, Purana Jubbal	
		15. Sanjaya Kumar, Purana Jubbal	5,186
		16. Rama Nand, Kiyari	
		17. Dinesh Kumar, Kiyari	
		18. Sandeep Kumar Mokhta, Kiyari *Jhaldi ra Deo*	
		19. Bala Nand Sharma, Salaokra (Pujari)	
		20. Mohar Singh, Jhaladi	
		21. Bhagat Ram, Jhaladi	
		22. Kunji Ram, Jhaladi	
		23. Jeet Singh, Jhaladi	
		*Offerings made in temples (*Chadhava*)* (and miscelleneous items)	
Grand Total	42,807		35,043
(The balance deposited with the cashier of the *Shadi ra Deo*)			

Conclusion

The essay reports social, economic and psychological evidence for developing an opinion that the institution of deity has vital role in mental health. It also suggests that there is need for modification in the institution in such a way that the interventions made are complementary to the nature of the institution. Such interventions are made by the natives of Himalaya in their struggle to save the environment, the Chipko Movement (Pirta, 2003). This requires an integrative approach to mental health as suggested by the biological, cultural and humanist pathways of human evolution (Figure 7.1).

Fig. 7.1: The three pathways of evolution: biological (P-1), cultural (P-2), and divine (P-3)

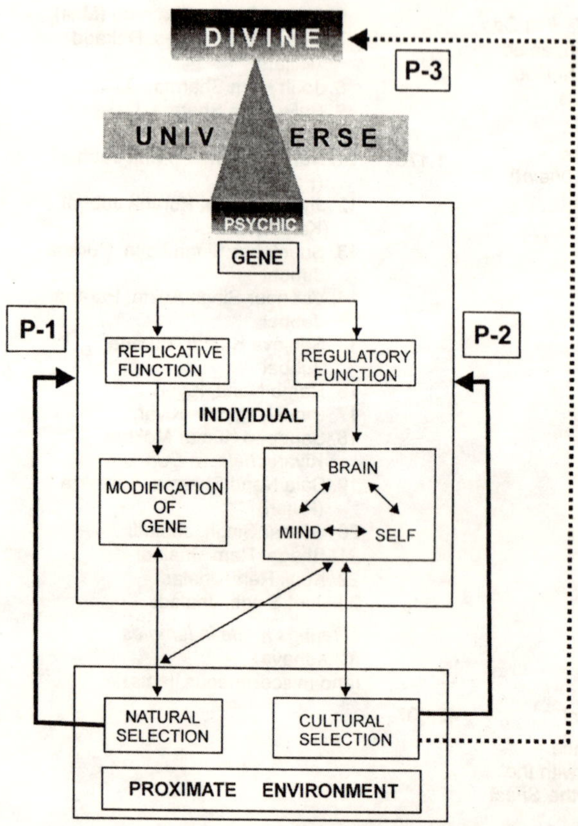

Our endeavour in rejuvenating the traditional system of mental hygiene has two objectives—in the first place we have to understand the socio-religious practices as the most recent evolutionary phenomenon specific to human species (the first transition from biological to mental), and our second objective is to understand the role of divine factor in mental health (the second transition from mental to divine). These transitions are exemplified in Sri Aurobindo's philosophy of integral yoga or the evolution of psychic being (Feys, 1973). Furthermore, the institution of deity is socio-religious and universal in nature, it has also evoked interest among the biologists. Some examples are, the socio-biological explanations of religious phenomena (Wilson, 1978), the biological and cultural co-evolution (Gadgil, 2001), and the explanatory models of possession and related behaviours (Crook, 1995).

It is important to identify these transitions in individual's cognition and behaviour. Our concern is to study the contextual basis of the transitions in the institution of deity. We are exploring these transitions among the natives of Shimla region. The mainstream psychology has not shown any keenness in the study of these mental phenomena. Perhaps they are challenging and defy measurement. In future, there is need to explore the survival value of these transitions for the individual as well as for the group.

Future Agenda

In this study the society and nature are not used to define a primeval relationship between the two. Neither there is any attempt here to study the relationship in historical terms. The aim is to present the existing state of the selective social and environmental issues in the North West Himalayas as perceived by the people including the scientists, politicians and planners and other intelligentsia. Although the emphasis was to develop a holist view of nature and society, the other two interactions—the human dominance over its environment and the natural constraints on the social system—cannot be undermined.

The first half of the book explains the major issues and problems in the three chapters: life and its support system, ecology and sustainability, social aspects of water, forest and land. The second half of the volume introduces some approaches and solutions related to sustainable development. It starts with the diversity of views and is followed by the study of cooperative relationships in three scenarios—the primate societies, the natives of Himalaya and the institution of deity.

We here summarize the issues and problems that are important and need further debate and research. The first section presents the problems and issues; second section suggests the need to strengthen local institutions keeping in view the global scenario; and, the third section calls for a cognitive revolution directed at human well-being.

Facing the Challenge

Since the understanding of the surrounding physical and social systems is dependent upon the cognitive and mental factors, an attribute of human species, there are chances of subjectivity or bias. The criterion to rectify this bias has to be worked out by human beings themselves.

This is the biggest dilemma when we talk about ecology and sustainability. Ecology refers to the relationship among the elements (natural and manmade) of the ecosystem whereas sustainability is the human constraint to maintain these relationships for our own survival and the survival of our future generations. This human constraint is almost entirely defined by the human beings as far as the most dominant views of environment are concerned.

A controversial problem that often figures in environmental debates is the limited land area and the growth of the human population. There is a loud cry about population explosion as a major problem for environment and development. It is in this area, particularly, that even the most venerable minds have fallen to Malthusian fallacy. They grossly undermine the human cognitive competence to solve problems. All limits of decency are crossed in suggesting barbaric ways to reduce the Darwinian fitness. At the same time there is large industry that survives by increasing the libidinal impulses of people. In such a scenario the demographic profile of Himachal Pradesh makes academicians complement its peasantry.

Though the limitless demands of humans may be an important factor contributing to large number of environmental problems, the most learned section of society grossly undermines it. Even the writers from the developing societies, whose needs are comparatively frugal, get entrapped in the jargon of materialistic fallacy—the happiness lies in the acquisition of more and more material goods. On the other side the mental nature of happiness and fulfillment is undermined. Moreover there is vociferous campaign to denigrate one's own culture and society. Little do we realize that the silent folks in hilly terrain of Himachal Pradesh have set an example by becoming the socially most progressive state in India.

This brings us to the issue of poverty and its presumed negative relationship with development and environment. It is rare to find writers who have negated this relationship. But at the same time it is difficult to find scientific data and methods to ascertain what poverty is and how it lowers the pace of development and deteriorates the environment. More important, however, is to know the causes of poverty. It is unique in this case that the planners, politicians and the enforcing agencies, by neglecting the role of psychological and social factors, have miserably failed. Rather they seem to propagate the colonization of mind of local people by the materialistic policies of the developed world.

There appears to be lack of sensitivity in our policies regarding scientific findings on the one hand and the needs of the people on the other. An example of this split in the contemporary India and particularly in Himachal Pradesh is the construction of large dams. The planners, politicians and enforcing agencies, in this case, have overlooked the science of ecology as well as the miseries of the displaced people.

Largely the policy of forest conservation has received only lip service from the planners and politicians; the emphasis has been to compel Himachal Pradesh to earn more money by exploiting its forest resources. However, it is here that the natives of Himalayas were able to persuade the most reluctant politicians for the sustainable use of forests. A major challenge, however, is to understand the dynamic relationship between forest, water and land, especially in the context of watershed development programmes.

Many now consider the cooperative nature of society as an important factor in sustainable development. In this report we have discussed the biological origin of cooperation from naturalist studies on the nonhuman primates. This may help in building a sound theoretical basis for developing a humanist view of a cohesive human group instead of a very simplistic "primal horde" on which the early anthropological and psychoanalytic assumptions of human society were formulated. This was followed by a success story of natives from Garhwal and Himachal for the protection of the Himalayan forests. This success story is now well known all over the world by the name Chipko or hug-the-tree movement.

Strengthening Local Institutions

The resilience of the hill people as a peculiar biological and cultural adaptation to the mountains of the Himalayan region is well known. However various large-scale interventions may increase the vulnerability of these people in the mountain ecosystem. This vulnerability would vary in different sections of society and along the dimension of gender and other social factors.

One consequence of these developmental changes in the Himalayas is probably associated with the psychological dimensions of the allostatic systems of people migrating due to push or pull factors. A social scientist would like to integrate the vulnerability and resiliency approach (Ray, 2004) with the holistic approach adopted here to understand the mental health of displaced populations. Migration is a global problem. The World Health Report 2001 on Mental Health mentioned a huge accumulation of the displaced persons particularly from their native areas. Moreover, the problem of displacement has several theoretically important issues. Two such issues pertain to the areas of effect and memory.

Furthermore, we can explore the institution of local deity in relation to the general well-being of people. In recent years a socio-ecologist, Crook (1997) has explored the indigenous psychiatry in some parts of Western Himalayas and found these culture specific mental phenomena, for example the possession by deities, interesting. On the contrary, it is difficult to understand the puritan attitude of social scientists towards these little traditions (Rao, 2001). At the same time, knowledge seekers would find the interaction of people with their forest gods, water spirits, ghosts and demons full of curious phenomena (Singh, 2003). The indifference of the academicians to such phenomena should not come in our way while we join the resistance against the Western colonization of mental health.

Our students are doing research in a stimulating environment but it lacks basic facilities needed for good quality research. There is immense need to strengthen the structure of collection and dissemination of information that is effective and within the reach of a research scholar. This orientation is essential from an early age, the graduation level. It would be too simplistic to assume that no research work is going on in the colleges, universities and other institutions of the State. However, the need is to share this information. Efforts are essential to boost the self-esteem of those who choose higher studies; in social sciences the scholars use own resources. Provision of grants would solve these twin problems.

Although Himachal Pradesh has dealt with the problem of literacy effectively and in a comparatively short time, now the time is to improve the quality at a higher level. Then only the State and its people may realize the benefits of its efforts. It certainly needs much less financial input from the State than the watershed of money on the livelihood schemes at the subsistence level. There is time to take a giant cognitive leap. The State has to orient its policies of borrowing money for watersheds towards generating watersheds of knowledge.

The Imperative of Cognitive Revolution

Human cognitive abilities can immensely enrich the niche by contributing to the repertoire of the habitat specific behaviours. There is however a tendency of dominance or use of power by other group to check it or compete with it. Therefore the "comparative advantage" starts diminishing. To counter the competitive strategies of the other groups there is need for a more superior cognitive innovation, a greater emphasis on more specialization in interactions between the people and their habitat. In other words there is competition between the "specialists" and the more dominant "generalists."

There seems to be a paradox, especially in context to the huge neocortical mass, that each individual possesses and its immense potential for cognitive innovations, which is a universal feature. On the other hand, there is a little use of this potential by a majority of population living on the subsistence level. The way to resolve the paradox is perhaps very clear, to make use of this immense potential for "specialization." But to achieve this, the route people choose is from specialists to generalists. Another path is from generalists to specialists. This is a path from whole to its parts, which needs experimentation.

An understanding of the global scenario is most important today for people when the cultural evolution has released the human species from its biological constraints. Now the human habitat is not narrow, as it was for the primitive human groups, its extent is the whole earth. If the people of Himachal Pradesh do not want to enlarge their habitat, they may do it at a great risk. Perhaps they do not have enough power to stop the others to graze their habitat. In this sense niche for modern human beings is only beneficial if they take benefit of the cognitive evolution and take a route from generalists to specialists.

People of Himachal Pradesh may choose to remain specialists but they will have to import experts, as is the present scenario. The cost is very heavy. Socially, the people are classified as poor, less developed and some times a burden of the more developed. Take for example watershed management and social forestry schemes. The State is borrowing huge amount of money and expert power even for these comparatively less complex cognitive activities.

Appendix 1

Moratorium on Commercial Felling of Trees in the Himalayas

S.P. Mukerji **Ministry of Agriculture**

Secretary

D.O. No. 8-128/81-FRY(COORD) June 3, 1983.

My dear Shri Srivastava,

You may recall that U.P. Government had appointed an Expert Committee under the Chairmanship of Dr. K.N. Kaul to study the policy on felling and protection of forests and maintenance of the environmental balance in the Himalayan Region. The report of this Committee as also the decisions taken by the Committee of Secretaries of Uttar Pradesh Government on this report were received in the ministry as well in the Department of Environment. The matter has been considered carefully by the Government of India. Their views are as follows:

(*a*) *Moratorium on commercial felling in the U.P. Hills*: Considering the serious ecological situation in the Himalayas there is urgent need for the moratorium on commercial felling in the U.P. Himalayas right down to the Siwalik foothills, irrespective of the considerations of altitude or gradient. This moratorium should apply to all forests, including reserved, protected civil, soyam, panchayat, khat, etc. The essential requirements of the people of those areas should, however, continuc to be met largely, from dead and dying trees or from trees on slopes of lower than 30°. This moratorium should extend, to allow for at least one growth cycle, for a period of 15 years. The situation may be reviewed after 10 years.

(*b*) *Need for massive afforestation programme with peoples participation during moratorium*: During the period of moratorium of forest exploitation, all possible efforts need to be directed by the Forest Department towards a massive afforestation program with peoples' full participation on the basis of careful conceived program inspired by experiments which have succeeded elsewhere.

(*c*) *Need for reorienting working plans into environmental sound "Action Plans" based on scientific research*: There is need for a total reorientation of the existing forest "Working Plans" into environmentally sound "Action Plans" on the basis of scientific research which should cover all types of forests and fit into an overall "management plans" for each watershed area based on optimum land-use considerations.

(*d*) *Community forests around villages managed by peoples' cooperative agencies*: An area of about 3 km around villages should be earmarked for raising plantations to meet the requirements of the people on a sustained basis for food, fuel, fodder, fibre, fertilizer and timber through program devised to involve the efforts of village communities. The existing civil, soyam, khat and panchayat forests should be managed through cooperative agencies, involving the Forest Department, the people and if necessary the industry.

(*e*) *Extension orientation for forest department*: The Forest Department needs to acquire a strong extension to motivate and channelise the peoples' efforts in massive agro and social forestry program with ecologically compatible species that fulfill peoples' needs.

(*f*) *Building up of information base through scientific studies:* The Forest Department needs to undertake relevant scientific studies for building up a strong information base to provide answers to various issues raised in the forests. These scientific studies should cover such parameters as crown density, altitude, gradients, geomorphology and state of the forests as a whole.

It is requested that action may now kindly be taken on the above lines and the ministry informed.

In this connection it is also brought to your notice that the Prime Minister has observed that many Members of Parliament are worried about the hardship to which poor people are put because of shortage of wood. She has further observed that the suggestion for extending the complete ban on felling of trees to all hill areas of U.P. should be reviewed to the extent that *availability of firewood for the local population* is assured by permitting very selective felling of dead and dying trees and those in slopes of less than 30°. The Kaul Committee had recommended a complete ban for identified sensitive areas, but if this is extended to the entire hill areas, at least those portions which were contributing to the firewood needs of the local population should be excluded.

You may also kindly examine this point carefully and communicate proposed action.

I would be grateful if you could send an early reply.

With kind regards,

Yours Sincerely,
sd/-
(S.P. Mukherjee)

Shri S.D. Srivastava,
Chief Secretary,
Government of Uttar Pradesh,
Lucknow.

Copy to: Shri J.C. Pant, Forest Secretary,
Government of Uttar Pradesh, Lucknow.

Appendix 2

Declaration of the Save Himalaya Movement

Aggressive development policy has created the crisis of survival for both—the Nature and the Man—in Himalaya. It has not only adversely affected the people of this area, but ten times more people have been affected because of disaster in Himalayas in the shape of floods, soil-erosion and draught.

This great mountain touches the boundaries of many countries and controls the climate of a large region. Besides material prosperity, Himalaya is the symbol of cultural inspiration and emotional integration. For human kind Himalaya has been the source of spiritual inspiration and peace. It has today become the center of ecological crisis, human misery and due to it of discontent and chaos. This has become an issue of global concern.

Policies based on the material civilization, instead of healing up the seriously wounded Himalaya, have accelerated the pace of exploitation of its water, forest and mineral resources. Construction of monstrous Tehri Dam is the symbol of this. This dam has been opposed continuously for last twenty years. This is economically bankrupt, socially disruptive, killer culture and ecologically disastrous. So to protect the economic, social, cultural and ecological values we will leave no stone upturned to stop it forthwith.

We are disturbed with a number of such dams, which are proposed to be constructed in Himalaya. Some of these projects are to supply power and water to big industries and cities (although for a very short period) by destroying the ecology of Himalayas and uprooting its inhabitants. The export of water—basic resource for survival—from this poor region is a grave injustice which will increase the regional imbalance. This is a legalized robbery. It is the primary duty of every citizen to stop it.

We in Himalayas are facing the crisis of survival due to suicidal activities being carried out in the name of development. These are—commercial exploitation of the forests, mining, construction of dams, which inundate vast areas and displace a large number of people, mechanical heavy explosions creating artificial tremors, construction of five star hotels for luxury tourism and multi-storeyed buildings. We call upon the people of Himalayas, lovers of Himalayas and those who believe in the dignity of human life to come forward to oppose these activities for their survival. The Uttarkashi Earthquake was warning to stop tampering with Himalayas, to which deaf ears were turned.

There is need of a new a long term policy for the protection of dying Himalayas. Following steps need to be taken forthwith to heal up its wounds and the development of the people.

1. Power generation from each and every stream, rivulet and river without flooding the cultivated land, forests and habitats, so that power may be easily available for lifting up the water and for ropeways without reliance on central grid. 20 per cent of power generated from big projects (as the five components in the production process—land, labour, capital, management and enterprise—should get their equal share) should be given free of cost to village (Gram Sabhas), block committees and district boards in the catchment area, so that it may be added to their meager incomes. For example, in this respect Uttarkashi district has the first right to get a share from the Maneri-Bhali hydel project, Stage-1.
2. Land use survey of all unirrigated hill slopes including reserve forest and civil forest land be done. Water should be provided to grow fruits, fodder and more trees on this land. Till these trees give returns, people should be provided employment, to plant and look after these trees. These trees will be the private property of the people and by giving them permanent employment the economy will strengthen. The plains will get fertile soil from the hills. The flow of the rivers will be regularized and the water problem will be permanently solved.
3. Local people should be given liberal aid to construct houses of the local type for the convenience of pilgrims, nature-lovers and those coming for the search of peace.

Conservation of places of scenic beauty and maintenance of roads to these spots should be done by those who are in control of the place.

4. Reclamation of slopes and land damaged by mining, road construction and debris of Tehri Dam.

We declare a Himalayan Policy in which the inspiring aspects of Himalayas is maintained. The wounds of this great mountain system be healed up, there should be economic development of the people and the natural resources of Himalayas should be utilized in a way in which future generations are benefited in a sustained manner without any harm to its fragile eco-system.

The main objectives of this policy should be:

1. Himalayas should remain a living space for the permanent residents, spiritual seekers, pilgrims, and tourists visiting for peace and enjoying scenic beauty.
2. Resources should be used for regional economic self-sufficiency. Ban on indiscriminate exploitation and export of resources (e.g. mining, deforestation and construction of big dams etc.).
3. To maintain the local landscape for a number of economic activities, specially for tourism connected with scenic beauty. 4. Some of the flora and fauna species of Himalayan region have become scarce; to preserve the genetic biodiversity of these.
5. More autonomy for the development of local institutions which is essential for the protection, utilization. carrying capacity, sustainability and cultural development. In this context, the formation of separate hill state of Uttarakhand should be done immediately.

Women bear the burden of hardships of hill life. Top priority should be given to lessen their miseries. For this:

1. Easy availability of fodder, fuel and water near the villages should be assured.
2. There should be prohibition, because liquor is destroying the health, happiness and prosperity of the hill-life.

3. In order to revive the family life, employment to all should be provided by lifting and conserving water on the hill tops, planting food, fodder, fiber trees on slopes and generating electricity from all rivulets.

(Passed in the Conference held near Tehri Dam site on May 13th, 14th and 15th 1992 and attended by more than 100 delegates from U.P. Hills and other States of India, as revised on Nov. 25th, 26th, 1995 at Khadi and Lakshmi Ashram, Kausani on Feb. 15th, 1996).

Appendix 3

National Parks and Sanctuaries in Himachal Pradesh*

Name	*District(s)*	*Area(km^2)*	*Notes (Forest Department 2003)*
National Parks			
Great Himalayan	Kullu	620.00	765.00 (increase)
Pin Valley	Lahul & Spiti	675.00	
Sanctuaries			
Bandli	Mandi	41.33	
Chail	Solan, Shimla	108.54	
Churdhar	Sirmaur, Shimla	56.15	66.00 (increase)
Daranghati	Shimla	167.40	
Darlaghat	Solan, Bilaspur	92.26	6.00 (decrease)
Gamgul Siahbehi	Chamba	108.85	
Gobind Sagar	Bilaspur	100.34	
Kais	Kullu	14.19	
Kalatop Khajjiar	Chamba	20.27	89.00 (increase)
Kanawar	Kullu	60.70	
Khokhan	Kullu	14.05	
Kugti	Chamba	378.87	
Lippa Asrang	Kinnaur	30.90	
Majathal	Solan, Shimla	39.39	
Manali	Kullu	31.80	
Naina Devi	Bilaspur	122.68	Shri Nainadevi
Nargu	Mandi	278.37	
Pong Lake	Kangra	307.29	Pongdam Lake
Rakchham Chhitkul	Kinnaur	34.11	304.00 (increase)
Renuka	Sirmaur	4.03	
Rupi Bhaba	Kinnaur	269.15	503.00 (increase)
Sechu Tuan Nala	Chamba	102.95	Sach-Tuan Nala
Shikari Devi	Mandi	72.00	

(*Contd.*)

* *Source*: Singh, Kothari & Pande, 1990.

(Contd.)

Name	District(s)	Area(km^2)	Notes (Forest Department 2003)
Shilli	Solan	2.13	
Shimla Water Catchment	Shimla	10.25	Water Supply Catchment
Simbalbara	Sirmaur	19.03	
Talra	Shimla	40.49	
Tirthan	Kullu	61.13	
Tundah	Chamba	64.22	
New Sanctuaries (*Forest Department 2003*)			
Dhauladhar	Kangra	944.00	
Kibber	Lahaul & Spiti	1400.00	
Sainj	Kullu	90.00	

Appendix 4

List of Some of the Plants Eaten by the Rhesus Monkey (R) and Hanuman Langur (L) in Himachal Pradesh*

Plant species	*Eaten by*	*Plant species*	*Eaten by*
Trees		Hymenodictyon excelsum	R.L
Abies pindrow	L	Juglans regia	L
Acacia arabica	R,L	Lannea coromandelica	R,L
A. catechu	R,L	Litsea monopetala	L
A. leucophlora	R,L	L. umbrosa	L
Acer caesium	L	Machilus duthiei	R,L
A. villosum	L	M. odoratissima	R,L
Aegle marmelos	R,L	Madhuca longifolia	R,L
Asculus indica	R,L	Mallotus philippinensis	R,L
Albizia chinesis	R,L	Mangifera indica	R,L
A. lebbek	R,L	Melia azedirach	R,L
Azadirachta indica	R,L	Morus alba	R,L
Bauhinia pupurea	R,L	M. serrata	R,L
B. recemosa	R,L	Myrica nagi	R,L
B. variegata	R,L	Ougeinia oojeinensis	R,L
Betula alnoides	R,L	Phoebe lanceolata	R,L
B. utilis	R,L	Pinus girardiana	R,L
Bombax ceiba	R,L	P. roxburghii	R
Butea monosperma	R,L	P. wallichiana	R
Casearia tomentosa	L	Pongamia pinnata	R,L
Castenia sativa	L	Populus ciliata	L
Cedrus deodara	R	Prunus armeniaca	R,L
Celtis australis	R,L	P. cerassoides	R,L
Cornus capitata	L	P. cornuta	R,L
C. macrophylla	L	Pyrus pashia	R,L
C. obloga	L	Quercus dilatata	R,L
Cordia dichotoma	R,L	Q. glauca	R,L
Corylus colurna	L		

(*Contd.*)

* Pirta, Gadgil & Kharshikar, 1997.

(*Contd.*)

Plant species	*Eaten by*	*Plant species*	*Eaten by*
Cotoneaster bacillaris	R,L	Q. leucotrichophora	R,L
Dalbergia sissoo	R,L	Q. semicarpifolia	R,L
Diploknema butyracea	R,L	Rhododendron arboreum	R,L
Ehretia laevis	R,L	R. companulatum	R,L
Emblica oficinalis	R,L	Robinia pseudoacacia	R,L
Ficus auriculata	R,L	Shorea robusta	R,L
F. bangalensis	R,L	Sterculia urens	L
F. glomerata	R,L	Syzygium cumini	R,L
F. palmate	R,L	Tamarandus indica	R,L
F. religiosa	R,L	Taxus baccata	L
Grevia elastica	R,L	Tectona grandis	R,L
G. optiva	R,L	Terminalia alata	R,L
G. sapida	R,L	T. belerica	R,L
G. tiliaefolia	R,L	T. chebula	R,L
Toona serrata	R,L	Pueraria tuberosa	L
Viburnum cotinifolium	R,L	Randia dumetorum	L
V. mullaha	R,L	Rosa moschata	R
Zanthoxylum armateum	R,L	Rubus biflorus	R,L
Ziziphus mauratiana	L	R. ellipticus	R,L
		R. niveus	R
Shrubs and climbers		Sapium sabiferum	R
		Smilex indica	R,L
Abrus precatorius	R	Solanum nigram	R,L
Adhatoda vasica	L	Solena ampexicaulis	R,L
Antidesma diandrum	R	Thevetia peruviana	L
Barleria cristata	L	Trifolium repens	R
Bauhinia vahlii	R,L	Urtica ardens	L
Berberis aristata	R,L	Vitis himalayana	R,L
Barsera serrata	L	Woodfordia frticosa	R,L
Capparis horrida	R,L	Zizyphus numularia	R,L
Carissa opaca	R,L		
Cissampelos pariera	R	**Grasses and other herbs**	
Clerodendron viscosa	L		
Cudrania cochinchinesis	R,L	Amdrosace umbellate	R
Desmodium gangeticum	L	Arisaema tortuosum	L
D. latifolium	L	Arundinella nepalensis	R
Diascorea bulbifera	R	Bupteurum hamittonii	R
Elschltozia polystachia	L	Callicarpa macrophylla	R
Flacourtia indica	L	Chenopodium album	R,L

(*Contd.*)

(*Contd.*)

Plant species	*Eaten by*	*Plant species*	*Eaten by*
Flemingia vestica	R,L	Chenopodium album	R,L
Ichnocarpus frutescens	R,L	Commelina obliqug	R,L
Indigofera girardiana	R,L	Cynodon dactylon	R,L
Jasminum multiforum	R,L	Diascorea belophylla	R,L
Lantana camara	R	Dicliptera roxburghii	R
Leguminosae puiraria	L	Diplazium frandosum	L
Leptadermis lanceolatus	L	Emilia sonchifolia	R
Ligustrum oleaceae	R,L	Fagopyrum dibotrys	R,L
Machilus lanceolata	L	Nasturtium officinale	R,L
Maclura cochinensis	L	Oplismensus compositus	R
Millettia auriculata	L	Oxalis corniculata	R
Murraya exotica	R,L	Polygonum barbatum	R
M. koenigii	R,L	Scindapsis officinalis	R
M. paniculata	L	Sida cordata	R
Ocimum bascilicum	L	Stellaria media	R
Physalis peruviana	L	Vicia sativa	R
Principea armeniaca	R.L	Zingiber roseum	R

Bibliography

Abdul Kalam, A.P.J., & Rajan, Y.S. (1998). *India 2020. A vision for the new millennium*. New Delhi: Penguin.

Alter, R.C. (2002). *Water for Pabolee. Stories about people and development in the Himalayas*. New Delhi: Orient Longman.

Anonymous (1991). Case study. Rehabilitation of Pong Dam oustees in hill areas of Himachal Pradesh. Resource group on Hill Area Development, H. P. Institute of Public Administration, Fairlawn, Shimla–171012.

Anonymous. (2000). Impact assessment study of socio-economic development programmes—A case study of Himachal Pradesh. New Delhi: Asia pacific Socio-Economic Research Institute.

Arunachalam, V. (2001). The science behind tradition. *Current Science, 80*, 1272-1275.

Bahuguna, S.L. (1974). *Chipko andolan*. Ramnagar, Saharanpur: Garhwal Sabha. (in Hindi)

Bahuguna, S.L. (1978). *Tehri ka vishal Bandh*. Tehri: Tehri Bandh Virodhi Sangharsh Samiti (in Hindi)

Bahuguna, S.L. (1982). Let the Himalayan forests live! *Science Today*, March.

Bahuguna, S.L. (Ed.) (1995). *Jan-Jan ki Ganga-maiya* (pp.17-22). Silyara, Tehri-Garhwal, U.P.: Chipko Information Centre.

Bahuguna, S.L. (1997). *Chipko Message. Save Himalaya Movement*. Ganga Himalaya Kuti, Tehri (Garhwal), U.P.: Chipko Information Centre.

Bajaj, J., & Srinivas, M.D. (1996). *Annam bahu kurveet*. Madras: Centre for Policy Research.

Baker, R. St. B. (1982). Chipko—hug to the tree people. In *The Chipko march*. Silyara, Tehri-Garhwal, U.P.: Chipko Information Centre.

Bandura, A. (2001). Social cognitive theory: An agentic perspective. *Annual Review of Psychology, 52*, 1-26.

Bandyopadhyay, J. (1992). Sustainability and survival in the mountain context. *Ambio, 21*, 297-302.

Bandyopadhay, S. (2001). Editorial. *Everyman's Science*, 35, 175-177.

Batola, B.S. (2003). Ontology of labour and participation of youth in the labour force in north east India or hauntology of strategic action in the periphery. In A. Saikia (Ed.), *Population, environment, and the challenge of development* (pp. 326-344). New Delhi: Akansha Publishing House.

Berreman, G.D. (1989). Chipko: a movement to save the Himalayan environment and people. In C. Borden (Ed.), *Contemporary Indian tradition* (pp. 239-266). Washington: Smithsonian Institution Press.

Berry, J.W., van de Koppel, J.M.H., Senechal, C., Annis, R.C., Bahuchet, S. Cavalli-Sforza, L.L., & Witkin, H.A. (1987). *On the edge of the forest: Cultural adaptation and cognitive development in Central Africa*. Lisse: Swets & Zeitlinger.

Bhati, J.P., Singh, R., Rathore, M.S., & Sharma, L.R. (1992). Diversity of mountain farming systems in Himachal Pradesh, India. In N.S. Jodha, M. Banskota and Tej Pratap (Eds.), *Sustainable mountain agriculture. Farmer's strategies and innovative approaches*, Volume 2, pp. 497-515. New Delhi: Oxford & IBH.

Bhatt, C.P. (1992). *The future of large projects in the Himalaya*. Nainital: PAHAR People's Association for Himalaya Area Research.

Bimal, M. (2003). Migratory goat and sheep rearing in Himachal Pradesh, India. In J.M. Suttie and S.G. Reynolds (Eds.), *Transhumant Grazing Systems in Temperate Asia*. Rome: FAO.

Bingeman, K., Gardner, J. & Sinclair, J. (2000). Resilience and the village forest commons in the context of economic and urban growth, Manali, H.P., India. IASCP Conference, Indiana University.

Bose, A. (2000). Demographic transition. www.india-seminar.com/2000/488/4888.bose.htm

Bora, R.S. (1996). *Himalayan migration: A study of the hill region of Uttar Pradesh*. New Delhi: Sage.

Bunyard, P. (Ed.) (1996). *Gaia in action*. Edinburgh: Floris Books.

Calder I.R . (2004). Forests and water - closing the gap between public and science perceptions. *Water Science & Technology, 49* (7), 39-53.

Carpenter, V. (1999). "I'm a stranger alone in my country again": The conflict between the self and society in Indian poetry of Octavio Paz and Allen Ginsberg. Paper Presented to the Society for Latin American Studies Postgraduates in Latin American Studies (PILAS) 1999 Conference, The Graduate Institute, The University of Hull, Hull, England (4-5 December 1999).

Chaitanya, K. (2000). Man, nature and cosmos in Vedic India. *The Ecologist, 30*, 21-24.

Chandel, N., & Pirta, R.S. (2003). Mental health of Bhakra Dam oustees. Unpublished manuscript, Department of Psychology, Himachal Pradesh University, Shimla 171005.

Chandra Mohan, N. (2003). Politics of economic liberalization in India. *Harvard Asia Quarterly*, Spring.

Chandrashekhar, M.B., Singh, S., & Roy, P.S. (2003). Geospatial modelling techniques for rapid assessment of phytodiversity at landscape level in western Himalayas, Himachal Pradesh. *Current Science, 84*, 663-670.

Chhatre, A. (2003). The mirage of permanent boundaries: Politics of forest reservation in the western Himalayas, 1875-97. *Conservation and Society, 1*(1), 137-159.

Chidananda, S. (1987). An appeal to save the ecology of the Himalayas. In *The Chipko Message* (pp. 1-3). Silyara, Tehri-Garhwal, Uttar Pradesh: Chipko Information Centre.

Chidananda, S. (1991). *The philosophy, psychology and practice of yoga.* Shivanandanagar: The Divine Life Society.

Cohen, A. (2000). Excess female mortality in India: The case of Himachal Pradesh. *American Journal of Public Health, 90*(9), 1369-1371.

Cranney, B. (2001). *Local environment and lived experience. The mountain women of Himachal Pradesh.* New Delhi: Sage.

Crook, J.H. (1970). Sources of cooperation in animals and man. *Social Science Information, 9*(1), 27-48.

Crook, J.H. (1989). Introduction: Socioecological paradigms, evolution and history: perspectives for the 1990s. In A. Standen and R.A. Foley (Eds.), *Comparative socioecology. The behavioural ecology of humans and other mammals* (pp. 1-36). London: Blackwell Scientific Publication.

Crook, J.H. (1995). Psychological processes in cultural and genetic coevolution. In E. Jones and V. Reynolds (Eds.), *Survival and religion: Biological evolution and cultural change* (pp. 45-110). London: John Wiley & Sons.

Crook, J.H. (1997). The indigenous psychiatry of Ladakh, part I: practice theory approaches to trance possession in the Himalayas. *Anthropology & Medicine*, 4, 289-307.

Crook, J., & Low, J. (1997). *The yogins of Ladakh.* Delhi: Motilal Banarsidass.

Crook, J., & Osmaston, H. (Eds.) (1994). *Himalayan Buddhist villages.* Delhi: Motilal Banarsidass.

Cross, J.G., & Guyer, M.J. (1980). *Social traps.* Ann Arbor: University of Michigan Press.

Dalal, A.K. (2001). Health psychology. In J. Pandey (Ed.), *Psychology in India revisited: Developments in the discipline.* Vol. 2. *Personality and health psychology* (pp. 356-411). New Delhi: Sage.

Dangwal, D.D. (2005). Commercialisation of forests, timber extraction and deforestation in Uttaranchal, 1815-1947. *Conservation and Society, 3*(1), 110-133.

Darwin, C. (1859). *Origin of species.* London: John Murray.

Denholm, J., & Jodha, N.S. (1992). Agroforestry as an option for mountain agricultural development. In N. S. Jodha, M. Banskota and Tej Pratap (Eds.), *Sustainable mountain agriculture. Farmer's strategies and innovative approaches*, Volume 2, pp. 773-790. New Delhi: Oxford & IBH.

Deutsch, M. (1973). *The resolution of conflict: Constructive and destructive processes.* New York: Yale University Press.

Dewan, M.L., & Rautela, P. (2001). *People's movement for Himalayan rejuvenation.* New Delhi: Concept Publishing Company. (Second Revised and Enlarged Edition).

Dharampal (1993). *Bhartiya chitta manas and kala.* Madras: Centre for Policy Studies.

Dreze, J., & Kingdon, G.G. (1999). School participation in rural India. *The Development Economics Discussion Paper Series, London School of Economics*, N. 8. pp. 1-43.

Dreze, J., & Sen, A. (2002). *India: Development and participation*. New Delhi: Oxford.

Fernandes, W., Das J.C., & Rao, S. (1989). Displacement and rehabilitation: An estimate of extent and prospects. In W. Fernandes & E. Ganguly Thukral (Eds.), *Development, displacement and rehabilitation: Issues for national debate* (pp. 62-88). New Delhi: Indian Social Institute.

Feys, J. (1973). *The philosophy of evolution in Sri Aurobindo and Teilhard de Chardin*. Calcutta: Firma K.L. Mukhopadhyay.

Frazer, J.G. (1926). *The worship of nature*. London: Macmillan.

Gadgil, M. (1991). Ecological organization of the Indian society. *I.C.S.S.R. News Letter, XXI(4)*, 1-9.

Gadgil, M. (2001). *Ecological journeys. The science and politics of conservation in India*. New Delhi: Permanent Black.

Gadgil, M., & Guha, R. (1993). *This fissured land. An ecological history of India*. New Delhi: Oxford. (Fifth impression: 1999).

Gadgil, M., & Guha, R. (1995). *Ecology and equity. The use and abuse of nature in contemporary India*. New Delhi: Penguin.

Gadgil, M., & Malhotra, K.C. (1983). Adaptive significance of the Indian caste system: An ecological perspective. *Annals of Human Biology, 10*, 465-478.

Gadgil, M., & Rao, P.R.S. (1998). *Nurturing biodiversity: An indian agenda*. Ahmedabad: Center for Environment Education.

Goldsmith, E. (1998). *The way. An ecological world-view*. Athens: The University of Georgia Press.

Gouri, Mudgal, S., Morrison, E., & Mayers, J. (2004). Policy influences on forest-based livelihoods in Himachal Pradesh, India. International Institute for Environment and Development, London. pp. 1-128.

Goswami, K., & Pirta, R.S. (2001). Creating environmental consciousness: An experimental study. *Psycho-lingua, 31(1)*, 63-67.

Goswami, K., & Pirta, R.S. (2002). An experimental study on inducing environmental concern in girl students. *Indian Journal of Applied Psychology, 39*, 5-8.

Guha, R. (1989). *The unquiet woods. Ecological change and peasant resistance in the Himalaya*. New Delhi: Oxford. (New Expanded Edition 1999)

Guleria, A.S. (1987). A strategy for eco-development in Himalayan region: Watershed approach. In Y.P.S. Pangtey and S.C. Joshi (Eds.), *Western Himalaya Vol. II Environment, problems and development* (pp. 692-701). Nainital: Gyanodaya Prakashan.

Gupta, P.K., & Joshi, B.C. (1987). In R.K. Sapru (Ed.), *Environment management in India* (Vol. I) (pp. 221-29). New Delhi: Ashish Publishing House.

Gupta, V., Surie, G., Javidan, M., & Chhokar, J. (2002). Southern Asia cluster: Where the old meets the new? *Journal of World Business, 37*, 16-27.

Hamilton, W.D. (1964). Genetical theory of social behaviour (I & II). *Journal Theoretical Biology*, *7*, 1-16 and 17-32.

Hardin, G. (1968). The tragedy of the commons. *Science, 162*, 1243-8.

Harlow, H.F., & Harlow, M.K. (1966). Affection in primates. *Discovery*, January.

Hoon, V. (1996). *Living on the move: Bhotiyas of the Kumaon Himlaya*. New Delhi; Sage Publications.

Immerzeel, W.W., Pradhan, S., & Bhagat, R.M. (2004). An eco-regional approach to agricultural land use planning in Himachal Pradesh, India using geographic information systems. AFTA/WCCA joint congress on it in Agriculture.

Ittelson, W.H.; Proshansky, H.M.; Rivlin, L.G.; & Winkel, G.H. (1974). *An introduction to environmental psychology*. New York: Holt, Rinehart and Winston.

Iyer, K.G., & Roy, U.P. (2005). *Watershed management and sustainable development*. New Delhi: Kanishka Publishers, Distributors.

Jayal, N.D. (1987). Drought, development and desertification. In R.K. Sapru (Ed.), *Environment management in India* (Vol. I) (pp. 267-72). New Delhi: Ashish Publishing House.

Joshi, N.V., Gadgil, M., & Patil, S. (1993). Exploring cultural diversity of the people of India. *Current Science*, 64: 10-17.

Joshi, P.K., Singh, S., Agarwal, S., & Roy, P.S. (2001). Forest cover assessment in western Himalayas, Himachal Pradesh using IRS 1C/1D WiFS data. *Current Science, 80*, 941-947.

Kakar, S. (2001). *The essential writings of Sudhir Kakar*. Delhi: Oxford.

Kapila, K. (2004). Conjuring marriage: State legislation and Gaddi kinship. *Contributions to Indian Sociology* (n.s.), *38*(3), 379-409.

Kaul, R., Hilaluddin, Jandrotia, J.S., & Gowan, P.J.K. (2004). Hunting of large mammals and pheasants in the Indian western Himalaya. *Oryx*, *38*(4), 1-6.

Kingston, J.V. (1998). Prologue. In B. Saraswati (Ed.) *The cultural dimension of ecology*, pp. xii-xv. New Delhi: Indira Gandhi National Centre for the Arts & D.K. Printworld.

Kosambi, D.D. (1975). *The culture and civilization of ancient India: A historical outline*. Delhi: Vikas Publishing House.

Krishnamurti, J. (2000). *The awakening of intelligence*. New Delhi: Penguin Books.

Kropotkin, P. (1914). *Mutual aid. A factor in evolution*. Boston: Extending Horizon Books. (First edition 1902)

Kulkarni, S., & Choe, M.K. (1998). Wanted and Unwanted Fertility in Selected States of India. National Family Health Survey, Subject Reports, No. 6. pp.1-32. Bombay: SNDT Churchgate.

Kumar, R., Singh, R.D., & Sharma, K.D. (2005). Water resources of India. *Current Science*, *89*, 794-811.

Kunwar, S.S. (Ed.) (1982). *Hugging the Himalayas. The Chipko experience*. Gopeshwar (Chamoli): Dasholi Gram Swarajya Mandal.

Lewin, K. (1948). *Resolving social conflicts*. New York: Harper.

Lorenz, K.Z. (1976). *King Solomon's ring*. London: Methuen. (First edition 1952)

Lovelock, J. (1979). *Gaia: A new look at life on earth*. New York: Oxford.

Malhotra, K.C., Chatterjee, S., Gokhale, Y., & Srivastava, S. (2001). *Culture and ecological dimensions of sacred groves in India*. New Delhi: Indian national Science Academy and Bhopal: Indira Gandhi Rashtriya Manav Sangrahalaya.

Marten, G.G. (2001). *Human ecology. Basic concepts for sustainable development*. London: Earthscan Publications.

Mehra, M. (2005). From presidents's desk. *Corporate Governance. International Journal for Enhancing Board Performance*, *5*(1), 2.

Mehta, P., & Sharma, R.K. (1987). Poverty and food availability in tribal areas of Chamba District in Himachal Pradesh. In Y.P.S. Pangtey and S.C. Joshi (Eds.), *Western Himalaya Vol. II Environment, problems and development* (pp. 503-08). Nainital: Gyanodaya Prakashan.

Mira Behn (1978). The one remedy. *Himalaya: Man and Nature, 2(6)*, 4-5.

Mishra, A. (1995). *Rajasthan ki rajat boondein*. New Delhi: Gandhi Shanti Pratishthan.

Mishra, R.C. (2000). Perceptual, learning, and memory processes. In J. Pandey (Ed.), *Psychology in India revisited: Developments in the discipline. Vol. 1. Physiological foundation and human cognition* (pp. 94-150). New Delhi: Sage.

Mishra, R.C., Sinha, D., & Berry, J.W. (1996). *Ecology, acculturation and psychological adaptation: A study of adivasis in Bihar*. New Delhi: Sage.

Mishra, R.C., & Tripathi, N. (1996). Reproduction of patterns in relation to children's weaving experiences. In J. Pandey, D. Sinha and D.P.S. Bhawuk (Eds.), *Asian contributions to crosscultural psychology* (pp. 138-50). New Delhi: Sage.

Misra, G., & Gergen, K.J. (2001). On the place of culture in psychological science. In A.K. Dalal & G. Misra (Eds.), *New directions in Indian psychology* (pp. 405-24). New Delhi: Sage.

Misra, M.K. (2003). Base line information on medicinal plants conservation and sustainable utilization. Sponsered by UNDP/GEF, MoEF, Government of India & Coordinated by Foundation for Revitalisation of Local Health Traditions (FRLHT).

Misra, V.N. (1994). An Indian perception. *Seminar, 415*, March.

Misra, V.N. (1995a). Ganga kiski ...! In S.L. Bahuguna (Ed.), *Jan-Jan ki Ganga-maiya* (pp. 14-16). Silyara, Tehri-Garhwal, U.P.: Chipko Information Centre. (in Hindi)

Misra, V.N. (1995b). Ganga ka shap kab utarega. In S.L. Bahuguna (Ed.), *Jan-Jan ki Ganga-maiya* (pp. 17-22). Silyara, Tehri-Garhwal, U.P.: Chipko Information Centre. (in Hindi)

Mohanty, S., & Nandakumar, V. (2005). Education trends in India: a look at the statistics. *Education Journal–Gender and Education*, February 17.

Mutharayappa, R., Choe, M.K., Arnold, F., & Roy, T.K. (1997). Son Preference and Its Effect on Fertility in India. National Family Health Survey Subject Reports, No. 3. Bombay: SNDT Churchgate.

Naess, A. (1989). *Ecology, community and lifestyle: Outline of an ecosophy.* New York: Cambridge University Press.

Nandy, A. (1998). Cultural frames for social transformation: A credo. In F. Dallmayr & G.N. Devy (Eds.), *Between tradition and modernity: India's search for Identity* (pp. 250-64). New Delhi: Oxford.

Narasimhan, T.N. (2005). Water: Science and society. *Current Science, 89*, 787-793.

Narayan, K. (1997). *Mondays on the dark night of the moon. Himalayan foothill folktales*. New York: Oxford University Press.

Norberg-Hodge, H. (1994). May a hundred plants grow from one seed. The ecological tradition of Ladakh meets the future. In M. Batchelor and K. Brown (Eds.), *Buddhism and ecology* (pp. 41-54). Delhi: Motilal Banarsidass.

Odum, E.P. (1996). *Ecology. A bridge between science and society.* Massachusetts: Sinauer Associates.

Paliwal, G.S., & Singh, S.S. (1987). Some aspects and prospects of plant conservation in Garhwal Himalaya. In Y.P.S. Pangtey and S.C. Joshi (Eds.), *Western Himalaya Vol. II Environment, problems and development* (pp. 678-83). Nainital: Gyanodaya Prakashan.

Pandey, J. (*2004*). Psychology in India enters the Twenty-first Century: Movement toward an indigenous discipline. In J. Pandey (Ed.), *Psychology in India revisited—Developments in the discipline. Volume 3: Applied social and organizational psychology* (pp. 342-70). New Delhi: Sage.

Parmar, Y.S. (1985). People and development of forest in Western Himalaya. *Himalaya: Man and Nature, 8*(12), 41-43.

Pirta, R.S. (1983). Cooperative behaviour in rhesus monkeys living in urban and forest areas. *Proceedings of the Indian Academy of Sciences (Animal Sciences), 92*,199-205.

Pirta, R.S. (1984a). Maintenance of cooperative life in forest and urban rhesus monkeys (*Macaca mulatta*). *Proceedings of the Indian Academy of Sciences (Animal Sciences), 93*, 83-89.

Pirta, R.S. (1984b). Cooperative behaviour in rhesus monkeys, (*Macaca mulatta*) living in urban and forest areas. I. Genesis. In M.L. Roonwal, S.M. Mohnot, & N.S. Rathore (Eds.), *Current primate researches* (pp. 271-83). Jodhpur (India): Zoology Department, Jodhpur University.

Pirta, R.S. (1990). Cooperation in urban macaques and langurs. Department of Science and Technology, Government of India, New Delhi (unpublished report).

Pirta, R.S. (1994). *Himalaya bachao*. Rajghat, Varanasi: Sarva Sewa Sangh Prakashan. (in Hindi).

Pirta, R.S. (2000). *Jaivik vividhata ki aor*. Amritsar: All India Pingalwara Charitable Society. (in Hindi)

Pirta, R.S. (2001). Environment: Ethics, search for quality of life. In M.G. Chitkara (Ed.) *Encyclopaedia of Buddhism: A world faith. Volume VIII. Global values* (pp. 107-20). New Delhi: A. P. H. Publishing Corporation.

Pirta, R.S. (2002). Comparative psychology: Understanding behaviour of non-human primates. *Psychological Studies, 46*(1-3), 25-37.

Pirta, R.S. (2003). Native cognition of sustainable development in the western Himalaya. *Psychological Studies*, *48*, 30-42.

Pirta, R.S. (2004). A holistic model of sustainable development: An Indian approach to environmental psychology. In K. Joshi and M. Cornelissen (Eds.), *Consciousness, Indian psychology and yoga* (pp. 379-390). New Delhi: Centre for Studies in Civilizations.

Pirta, R.S., & Agrawal, A. (2003). The problem of forcibly displaced people and the psychological solution of rehabilitation. *Journal of Community Guidance and Research, 20*, 13-24.

Pirta, R.S., Gadgil, M., & Kharshikar, A.V. (1997). Management of the rhesus monkey *Macaca mulatta* and Hanuman langur *Presbytis entellus* in Himachal Pradesh, India. *Biological Conservation, 79*, 97-106.

Pirta, R.S., & Negi, V.S. (1996). Enriching the noosphere: Lessons from the Wheel of Life. In *Tabo monastery Millennium Celebrations 1996*. Souvenir. Shimla: Department of Language and Culture Himachal Pradesh, pp. 61-68.

Pirta, R.S., & Negi, V.S. (2000). The wheel of life and the noosphere. In M.G. Chitkara (Ed.), *Encyclopaedia of Buddhism: A world faith. Vol. IV. Buddhism and environment* (pp. 391-423). New Delhi: A.P.H. Publishing Corporation.

Prabhu, P. (2005). The right to live with dignity. *Seminar*, 552, 14-19.

Prakash, S. (1997). Poverty and Environment Linkages in Mountains and Uplands: Reflections on the 'Poverty Trap' Thesis. CREED Working Paper No. 12, Cornell University, New York, USA.

Prakash, S. (1998). Social institutions and common property resources in the mountains. *Mountain Research and Development*, *18*, 1-3.

Prasun, K. (Ed.) (1996). *Beejon ki virasat*. Khadi, Tehri Gehwal: Chipko Prakashan. (in Hindi)

Pyarelal (1959). *Towards new horizons*. Ahmedabad: Navjivan Publishing House.

Rajamani, V. (2005). Biological management of water on land. *Current Science*, *89*, 850-852.

Shabab, D. (1996). *Kullu. Himalayan abode of the divine*. New Delhi: Indus.

Rao, K.R. (2001). Consciousness studies: A survey of perspectives and research. In J. Pandey (Ed.), *Psychology in India revisited—Developments in the discipline. Volume 2: Personality and health psychology* (pp. 19-162). New Delhi: Sage.

Ranchan, S.P. (2001). *Aurotherapy: An alternate therapy system*. Delhi: Indian Publishers Distributors.

Ranchan, S.P., and Justa, H.R. (1981). *Folk tales of Himachal Pradesh*. Bombay: Bharatiya Vidya Bhavan.

Rangan, H. (2001). *Of myths and movements: Rethinking Chipko into Himalayan history*. New Delhi: Oxford.

Ray, O. (2004). How the mind hurts and heals the body. *American Psychologist, 59*(1), 29-40.

Rock, I., & Palmer, S. (1990). The legacy of Gestalt Psychology. *Vigyan Scientific American*, December.

Roonwal, M.L. (1976). Dominance behaviour in South Asian Primates. *Journal of Scientific and Industrial Research, 35*, 244-260.

Rotnenberg, D. (1993). The life of Arne Dekke E. Naess: from mountaintop to the depths of ecology. *National Geographic Journal of India, 39*, 13-23.

Roy, A. (1999). *The greater common good.* Bombay: India Book Distributors.

Roy, U.P., & Iyer, K.G. (2005). Participatory rural appraisal: Techniques for participatory planning and action. In K.G. Iyer and U.P. Roy (Eds.), *Watershed management and sustainable development*, pp. 166-72. New Delhi: Kanishka Publishers, Distributors.

Saberwal, V.K. (1999). *Pastoral politics. Shepherds, bureaucrats, and conservation in the western Himalaya.* New Delhi: Oxford University Press.

Saran, R. (2004). India's best and worst states. *India Today*, August 16.

Sarla Devi (1980). A blue-print for survival of the hills. *Supplement to Himlaya: Man and Nature, 4*(6), 1-16.

Sarala Devi (1982). *Revive our dying planet.* Nainital: Gyanodaya.

Sarin, M. (1996). *Joint forest management. The Haryana experience.* Ahmedabad: Centre for Environment Education.

Schmandt, J., & Ward, C.H. (2000). *Sustainable development: The challenge of transition.* Cambridge, U.K.: Cambridge University Press.

Scott, C.A., & Walter, M.F. (1993). Local knowledge and conventional soil science approaches to erosional processes in the Shivalik Himalaya. *Mountain Research and Development, 13*, 61-72.

Segall, M.H., Dasen, P.R., Berry, J.W., & Poortinga, Y.H. (1999). *Human behaviour in global perspective*. London: Allyn & Bacon.

Sen, A. (1995). Authoritarianism vs. cooperation: Perspectives on population policy. *Frontline*, October 6; October 20; November 3.

Sen, A. (1997). Radical needs and moderate reforms. In J. Dreze and A. Sen (Eds.), *Indian development: Selected regional perspectives* (pp. 1-32). New Delhi: Oxford.

Sen, A. (1999). *Inequality reexamined.* New Delhi: Oxford.

Sen, A. (2001). Many faces of gender inequality. *Frontline*, October 27-November 9.

Sen, R. (2003). *We the billion: A socio-psychological perspective on India's population.* New Delhi: Sage.

Sethi, Z., & Pirta, R.S. (2001). People's perception of polythene bags in Shimla: Humanistic and authoritarian approaches. Unpublished manuscript, Department of Psychology, Himachal Pradesh University, Shimla.

Shah, A. (1998). *Ecology and the crisis of overpopulation. Future prospects for global sustainability*. Cheltenham, UK: Edward Elgar.

Sharma, B.R. (2000). Sacred groves and their role in social life in Himachal Himalayas. Abstract *National Workshops on Community Strategies on the Management of natural Resources*. Bhopal.

Sharma, S. (1994). Psychology in India: major challenges. *The Indian Journal of Social Science, 7*(2), 179-188.

Sharma, S., & Ahuja, T. (1981). A study of field-dependence- independence in high school students as a function of sex, academic achievement and rural-urban habitat. *Personality Study & Group Behaviour, 2*(1), 11-19.

Sharma, S., & Ahuja, T. (1990). Antecedents of psychological differentiation. *Journal of Personality & clinical Studies, 6*(2), 185-192.

Sharma, S. Dogra, R. (1988). A study of field-dependent-independent cognitive styles in Indian and Tibetan boys and girls. *Personality Study & Group Behaviour, 8*(2), 1-6.

Shiva, V., & Bandyopadhyay, J. (1986). The evolution, structure, and impact of the Chipko Movement. *Mountain Research and Development, 6*, 133-142.

Shrestha, A.B. & Mishra, R.C. (1996). Sex differences in cognitive style of Brahmin and Gurung children from the hills and plains of Nepal. In J. Pandey, D. Sinha & D.P.S. Bhawuk (Eds.), *Asian contributions to crosscultural psychology* (pp. 166-74). New Delhi: Sage.

Singh, C. (1998). *Natural premises: Ecology and peasant life in the Western Himalaya 1800-1950*. Delhi: Oxford.

Singh, C. (2001). The search for sustainable development in the Himalayas. An interview with environmentalist Raghubir Singh Pirta. *Mountain Research and Development, 21*, 30-33.

Singh, C. (2001). The *Dhoom* in Himachal Pradesh: Community consciousness, peasant resistance or political resistance or political intrigue. In L. S. Thakur (Ed.) *Where mortals and mountain gods meet. Society and culture in Himachal Pradesh*, pp. 107-16 . Shimla: Indian Institute of Advanced Studies.

Singh, K., & Ballabh, V. (1996). *Cooperative management of natural resources*. New Delhi: Sage.

Singh, K.S. (2002). *People of India. Introduction*. New Delhi: Oxford. (Revised Edition)

Singh, R., Misra, S.M., Shyamananda, R.K., Sharma, G., Mahajan, I., & Aggarwal, B.K. (1987). Morphometry and catchment study of Renuka lake, Himachal Pradesh, India with a note on its flora and fauna. In Y.P.S. Pangtey and S. C. Joshi (Eds.), *Western Himalaya Vol. II Environment, problems and development* (pp. 639-49). Nainital: Gyanodaya Prakashan.

Singh, S.D. (1969). Urban monkeys. *Scientific American*, July.

Singh, S., Kothari, A., & Pande, P. (1990). *Directory of national parks and sanctuaries in Himachal Pradesh. Management status and profiles*. New Delhi: Indian Institute of Public Administration.

Singh, U. (2003). *Between worlds: Travels among mediums, shamans and healers*. New Delhi: Penguin.

Sinha, J. (1958). *Indian psychology. Volume I Cognition*. Delhi: Motilal Banarsidass. (Reprint 1986).

Sivananda, S. (1994). *Mind—its mysteries and control*. Shivanandanagar: The Divine Life Society.

Srinivas, M.N. (2002). Foreword. In K. S. Singh, *People of India: Introduction*, pp. vii-xvi. New Delhi: Oxford University Press. (Revised Edition)

Strong, M. (2001). Foreword. In G. G. Marten *Human ecology. Basic concepts for sustainable development*, pp. xii-xiii. London: Earthscan Publications.

Subramanya, K. (2005). *Engineering hydrology*. New Delhi: Tata McGraw-Hill.

Swarup, R., & Chand, K.P. (1987). *Management of social forestry in India with special reference to Himachal Pradesh*. New Delhi: Agricole Publishing Academy.

Thakar, V. (1989). *On an eternal voyage*. Ahmedabad: Vimal Prakashan Trust.

Thakur, K. (1997). *Environmental protection law and policy in India*. New Delhi: Deep & Deep publications.

Thakur, R. (1986). Tapovan. In S.L. Bahuguna (Ed.), *Hamare van hain jeevan pran* (pp.14-34). Tehri-Garhwal, U.P.: Parvatiya Navjivan Mandal. (in Hindi)

Thapar, R. (2002). *Early India. From the origins to AD 1300*. London: Penguin Books.

Tikekar, I. (1988). *Shrimad Bhagvat. Aik yuganukool darshan*. New Delhi: Acharya Kakasaheb Kalelkar Smarak Nidhi. (in Hindi)

Tinbergen, N, (1976). Ethology in a changing world. In P.P.G. Bateson and R.A. Hinde (Eds.) *Growing points in ethology*. London: Cambridge University Press.

Tiwari, S., & Bose, S. (2003). Low Base Flows and Livelihoods in India.*Internal Report II of a research project funded by the United Kingdom Department for International Development (DFID) R8171 Forestry Research Programme.*

Tripathi, R.C. (2002). Aligning development to values in India. In A.K. Dalal & G. Misra (Eds.), *New directions in Indian psychology* (pp. 307-325). New Delhi: Sage.

Valdiya, K.S. (1992). Must we have high dams in the geodynamically active Himalayan domain? *Current Science, 63*, 289-296.

Varadarajan, V. (1998). Presidential remarks. In D. Balasubramanian & N. Appaji Rao (Eds.), *The Indian human heritage* (pp. iv). Hyderabad: Universities Press.

Vedeld, T. (2005). Challenges to participatory watershed development in the Himalayan foothills. In K.G. Iyer and U.P. Roy (Eds.), *Watershed management and sustainable development* (pp. 135-151) New Delhi: Kanishka Publishers, Distributors.

Verma, L.R. (1998). *Indigenous technology knowledge for watershed management in upper north-west Himalayas of India*. Kathmandu, Nepal: Participatory Watershed Management Training in Asia (PWMTA) Program (GCP/RAS/161/NET, FAO (UN), U.N. Bldg., P.O. Box 25).

Verma, L.R., & Pratap, T. (1992). The experiences of an area-based development strategy in Himachal Pradesh, India. In N. S. Jodha, M. Banskota and Tej Pratap (Eds.), *Sustainable mountain agriculture. Farmer's strategies and innovative approaches* (Volume 2; pp. 609-36). New Delhi: Oxford & IBH.

Verma, V. (1996). *Gaddis of Dhauladhar. A transhumant tribe of the Himalayas*. New Delhi: Indus.

Vidyarthi, L.P. (1963). *The Maler: A study in nature-man-spirit complex*. Calcutta: Bookland.

Weber, T. (1988). *Hugging the trees: The story of the Chipko Movement*. New Delhi: Viking Press.

Wilson, E.O. (1978). *On human nature*. Cambridge, Massachusetts: Harvard University Press.

World Health Organization (2001). *The World Health Report: 2001: Mental health: new understanding, new hope*. Geneva

Zobel, D.B. (1987). Recognizing symptoms of stress in Himalayan ecosystems. In Y.P.S. Pangtey and S.C. Joshi (Eds.), *Western Himalaya*, Vol. II *Environment, problems and development*, (pp. 657-68). Nainital: Gyanodaya Prakashan.

Zoller, C.P. (1990). Aspects of traditional relations between man and environment in Bangan (North-western Garhwal). In N.K. Rustomji and C. Ramble (Eds.), *Himalayan environment and culture* (pp. 159-72). New Delhi: IIAS, Shimla and Indus.

Index